The Official Game Guide

John Whitman

HarperEntertainment
An Imprint of HarperCollinsPublishers

HarperEntertainment
An Imprint of HarperCollins*Publishers*
10 East 53rd Street, New York, NY 10022–5299

ISBN 0-06-107185-4

Book design and composition by Diane Hobbing of Snap-Haus Graphics

Book production by Bill Schiffmiller and Keith Conover

First printing: June 2000

Printed in the United States of America

Visit HarperEntertainment on the World Wide Web at www.harpercollins.com

10 9 8 7 6 5 4 3 2 1

CONTENTS

Congratulations! You've just Digivolved to the next level of Digimon excitement—the Digimon Digi-Battle Card Game! Now there's a whole new way to test your Digimon against the toughest competition, and this strategy guide will give you terrific tips to be the best!

Inside you'll find the following helpful hints and sections:

Rules of the Game A complete explanation of the rules of the Digimon Digi-Battle Card Game, from placing your Rookie card to combat on the Battle Deck to raking in the points!

Power Option Cards
A complete list of the Power Option cards and how they can take you to victory.

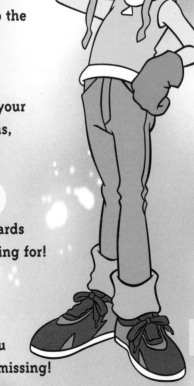

Digi-Hints: Tips for helping your creature Digivolve from a Rookie into the most powerful Champion possible.

Quick Reference Guide
A chart that shows you all the ways your Rookies can Digivolve into Champions, Ultimates, and Megas!

Bonus Section— Digimon Trading Cards!
Get a sneak preview of the trading cards everyone else is going to be scrambling for!

Digi-Appendix— Digimon Digi-Battle Game Cards Checklist
Check off the Digi-Battle cards as you get them, and find out what you're missing!

The First Byte

This first part of the book should answer your basic questions about the Digimon Digi-Battle Card Game. Don't worry if you still don't understand everything after this section—there's a lot more detail in the pages that follow!

Let's start at the beginning: What is a Digimon?

Digimon stands for "Digital Monster." Digimons live in the Digi-World. You can match them up in battles to see which one is the strongest, and with your help, your Digimons can digivolve into bigger, better, and stronger creatures.

Digimon started out as an electronic pocket game where two Digimon-owners competed against one another. But let's face it, tough characters like Greymon are hard to keep locked inside a little device. Pretty soon Digimons broke loose and started appearing on television, trading cards, and in this card game.

What do you need to play Digimon Digi-Battle Card Game?

Not much. Check out the list!

• Two players
• Each player needs a deck of 30 Digimon game cards.
• Game mat
• Score counter

That's it. No infrared beams. No downloaded programs from a satellite in geosynchronous orbit. No tech support. No problems!

If it's not electronic, how do the Digimons battle each other?

Digimon Digi-Battles in the card game aren't battery-powered—they're brain-powered! You use your smarts to assemble the best Digi-deck of cards you can. Or you and your opponent can decide to pick your decks randomly. Either way, this Game Guide comes in handy when you face off against your opponent using the game mat.

Each Digi-Battle card shows you how much Power each Digimon has—but you get to use special cards called Power Option cards to pump your Digimon up or to give it special powers.

How do you win the game?

At the end of each game, the cards show you how many points the winner earns. The first player to score 1,000 points wins the game.

A. SET-UP

1. Create a Battle Deck of 30 cards.
2. Select Rookie from Battle Deck, place down on Duel Zone.
3. Shuffle cards, deal yourself 10, place remaining 19 face down Online.
4. Each player turns over Rookie.
5. Note opponent's Battle Type. Compare Digimon Power.
6. Place Champion with correct Digivolve Requirements face down on Digivolve Zone.

B. DIGIVOLVE

1. Flip a coin to decide who goes first.
2. First player turns over card on Digivolve Zone, places it face up on top of card on Duel Zone. Fulfil any Requirements to complete turn.
3. Second player responds by Digivolving as above or saying, "Pass." If a player passes with a card face down on Digivolve Zone, he must move it Offline ("Use it, or lose it.")
4. You may Digivolve only one level per Duel, Player with no card to Digivolve must pass. If neither can Digivolve, proceed to **BATTLE**

C. BATTLE

1. Take turns playing Power Option cards to Power Port, one card per turn, keeping track of changes in Digimon Power.
2. Continue until a player runs out of options, or decides to stop, and says, "Pass." Other player may continue to play Power Option cards until he runs out or passes.
3. Compare Digimon Power to determine winner.
4. Winner scores points based on Digivolve level of loser, as shown in Score section at bottom of winning card.
5. Winner keeps all Digimons on Duel Zone. Loser sends all Digimons, except Rookie, Offline. Offline all Power Option cards.

D. RE-GROUP

1. Restore hand to 10 by drawing from Online deck. (You may first discard as many cards to Offline as you wish.)
2. When Online deck is down to zero, now or at any time during game, send all cards on your side of the board, except Rookie, Offline. Shuffle and return them face down to Online. To re-group, draw as many as needed to restore your hand to 10 cards.
3. You may change Rookie (place new Rookie face down on old Rookie on Duel Zone), and may place next-level Digimon face down on Digivolve Zone.
4. Last winner starts new Duel by returning to **DIGIVOLVE**, step #2.

POWER PORT

DUEL ZONE

ONLINE

OFFLINE

DIGIVOLVE ZONE

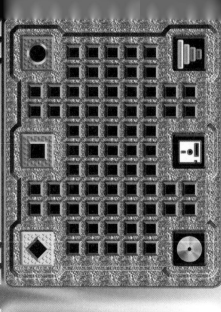

DIGIMON
DIGITAL MONSTER
DIGI-BATTLE CARD GAME

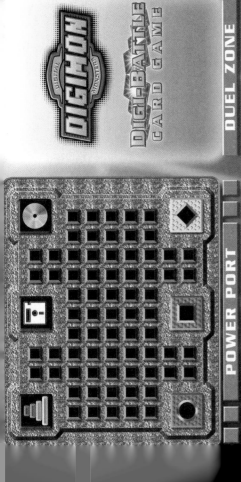

ONLINE

OFFLINE

DUEL ZONE

DIGIVOLVE ZONE

POWER PORT

RULES

A. SETUP
1. Create a Battle Deck of 30 cards.
2. Select Rookie from Battle Deck, place face down on Duel Zone.
3. Shuffle cards, deal yourself 10, place remaining 19 face down Online.
4. Each player turns over Rookie.
5. Note opponent's Battle Type. Compare Digimon Power.
6. Place Champion with correct Digivolve Requirements face down on Digivolve Zone.

B. DIGIVOLVE
1. Flip a coin to decide who goes first.
2. First player turns over card on Digivolve Zone, places it face up on top of card on Duel Zone. Fulfill any Requirements to complete turn.
3. Second player responds by Digivolving as above, or saying, "Pass." If a player passes with a card face down on Digivolve Zone, he must move it Offline. ("Use it, or lose it.")
4. You may Digivolve only one level per Duel. Player with no card to Digivolve must pass. If neither can Digivolve, proceed to **BATTLE**.

C. BATTLE
1. Take turns playing Power Option cards to Power Port, one card per turn, keeping track of changes in Digimon Power.
2. Continue until a player runs out of options, or decides to stop, and says, "Pass." Other player may continue to play Power Option cards until he runs out or passes.
3. Compare Digimon Power to determine winner.
4. Winner scores points based on Digivolve level of loser, as shown in Score section at bottom of winning card.
5. Winner keeps all Digimons on Duel Zone. Loser sends all Digimons, except Rookie, Offline. Offline all Power Option cards.

D. RE-GROUP
1. Restore hand to 10 by drawing from Online deck. (You may first discard as many cards to Offline as you wish)
2. When Online deck is down to zero, now or at any time during game, send all cards on your side of the board, except Rookie, Offline. Shuffle and return them face down to Online. To re-group, draw as many as needed to restore your hand to 10 cards.
3. You may change Rookie (place new Rookie face down on old Rookie on Duel Zone), and may place next-level Digimon face down on Digivolve Zone.
4. Last winner starts new Duel by returning to **DIGIVOLVE**, step #2.

Opening the Box

Okay, when you get your Digimon Digi-Battle Card Game, the first thing you do is rip off the plastic shrink-wrap stuff.

Inside you'll find the following items:

Game Mat

Starter Set of Game Cards

Score Counter

The Rules

DIGI-BATTLE CARD GAME

GAME MAT

This is where you're going to Duel it out with your opponent. The two sides of the board are exactly the same, so let's just have a look at one side.

Power Port. This is where you'll play your Power Option cards. It's where you get to say "Ha! I've got you now!"

Duel Zone. This is where the action takes place. You'll start here by putting down a Rookie card, but with luck you'll end by Digi-blasting your opponent's Digimon.

Online. This is where you put your cards until you're ready to use them. You can think of it as your storehouse of secret weapons.

700 800 900 1000 600 0 500 100 400 200 300

Rules. Always handy.

Digivolve Zone. This is where you'll play your Digivolve cards to pump your Digimon up to the next level and hopefully put your opponent in his or her place.

Offline. This is where you store your cards until you're ready to put them into action—it's where you put your cards after you've used them, or when you have to give up cards in order to use a special Power.

STARTER SET OF GAME CARDS

Okay, the board's cool, but let's face it, it just sits there. The cards are where the action is. That's because you get to arrange cards any way that you want.

The Starter Set contains 62 cards, including 48 Digimon cards and a mix of Power Option and Digivolve cards. Starter cards are all marked with an ST in the top right corner followed by a number. For example, the Rookie Agumon is part of the Starter Set, so his card number is ST—01.

BOOSTER CARDS

More Digimon cards are on the way! Booster cards come in packs of 8 with a random mix of new Digimon cards and additional Power Option cards. These cards will help you increase the power of your own personal Battle Deck. Booster cards are marked with a BO in the top right corner.

Check out the Digi-Appendix for pictures of all of the game cards in the Starter Set, plus Booster Sets #1 and #2.

St-01

Rookie Level

Begin Digivolve

Agumon

1st Edition

● 140 DEFEND
■ 230 CLAW ATTACK
◆ 380 PEPPER BREATH

Reptile Digimon
Vaccine

SCORE R:100 C:200 U:300 M:400

© Akiyoshi Hongo • Toei Animation   © 1999 BANDAI

Digimon Cards: Read 'em or Weep!

Here's how to read a Digimon card. We're going to use Greymon as an example.

DIGIMON LEVEL

This is pretty straightforward. You'll find your Digimon's level at the very top of the card. The Digimon levels are, from weakest to strongest:

Rookie

Champion

Ultimate

Mega

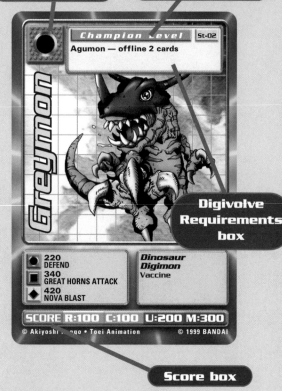

Battle Type

Digimon Level

Champion Level   St-02
Agumon — offline 2 cards

Digivolve Requirements box

220 DEFEND
340 GREAT HORNS ATTACK
420 NOVA BLAST

Dinosaur Digimon
Vaccine

SCORE R:100 C:100 U:200 M:300

© Akiyoshi Hongo • Toei Animation   © 1999 BANDAI

Score box

As you can see, Greymon is a Champion.

DIGIVOLVE REQUIREMENTS BOX

This is where you pay to play, so to speak. This box will tell you how many cards you must give up, or "Offline," in order to Digivolve to this level from Rookie level.

For instance, Greymon Digivolves from the Rookie Agumon. In order to do this, you must move two of your other cards from the Online stack to the Offline stack.

Sometimes, a Champion can Digivolve from more than one Rookie level. Check out Garurumon.

Gabumon card

Rookie Level · St-05

Begin Digivolve

1st Edition

Reptile Digimon
Data

- ● 350 BLUE BLASTER
- ■ 240 HORN ATTACK
- ◆ 150 DEFEND

SCORE R:100 C:200 U:300 M:400

© Akiyoshi Hongo • Toei Animation   © 1999 BANDAI

Tapirmon card

Rookie Level · Bo-36

Begin Digivolve

Animal Digimon
Vaccine

- ● 140 DEFEND
- ■ 220 DELETING VIRUS
- ◆ 350 WAKING DREAM

SCORE R:100 C:200 U:300 M:400

© Akiyoshi Hongo • Toei Animation   © 1999 BANDAI

Garurumon card

Champion Level · St-06

Gabumon — offline 2 cards
Tapirmon — offline 1 card

1st Edition

Animal Digimon
Data

- ● 410 HOWLING BLASTER
- ■ 330 SLAMMING ATTACK
- ◆ 180 DEFEND

SCORE R:100 C:100 U:200 M:300

© Akiyoshi Hongo • Toei Animation   © 1999 BANDAI

Two different Rookies, Gabumon and Tapirmon, can both Digivolve into Garurumon. However, Gabumon must Offline two cards to get there, while Tapirmon needs only one.

Naturally, Rookie Digimons don't require anything. Every Rookie card has the words "Begin Digivolve" in this box.

BATTLE TYPE

Digimons are divided into three Battle Types: Red (circle), Green (square), and Yellow (diamond).

You can find the Battle Type of any Digimon by checking the top left corner of its card.

Once you know what Battle Type your opponent is, you can see how much Digimon Power your creature has against it by checking the Power Chart at the bottom left corner. Let's check out Greymon as an example.

Greymon is a Red Battle Type. Check down at the bottom left corner. That's the Power Chart. It tells you that when Greymon faces another Red Battle Type, he delivers 220 Power units. Against a Green Battle Type, he delivers a pretty hefty 340 Power units. And against a Yellow Battle Type he pours out an awesome 420 points.

SCORE BOX

Last but not least, there's the Score section at the bottom of the card. If you win a Digi-Battle, this section tells you how many points you earn, depending on who you fought. For instance, if Greymon beats a Rookie (R), he earns 100 points. If he beats a Champion (C), he earns 100. Defeating an Ultimate (U) gets him 200, and putting away a Mega (M) earns him 300 points. You need a total of 1,000 points to win the game.

1

Rules of the Game

If you've played Digimon before, you probably already know the rules. Don't skip this section, though, because it's got some helpful hints.

Here's how to play:

Setup

1. **Create a Battle Deck of thirty cards.**

There are two ways to do this.

Flip a coin to see who gets to deal thirty cards randomly to each player.

If you and your opponent agree, you can choose your own premade Battle Deck. To create your own Battle Deck, please see "Building Your Personal Battle Deck" on page 56.

You *cannot* have duplicate cards. If you get a duplicate randomly, put it back and choose another card.

2. **Select two Rookie cards from the Battle Deck, place them facedown on the Duel Zone.**

Do you have more than one Rookie in your Battle Deck? If you answered yes, then check the rest of the deck to see which Rookie you can most easily Digivolve to the next level. Believe it or not, this is where the strategizing begins, so choose wisely.

3. **Shuffle cards, deal yourself ten, place remaining nineteen facedown Online.**

This is a random selection of ten cards. Hopefully, you have gotten a card you can use to Digivolve the Rookie you put in the Duel Zone.

4. Each player turns over Rookie.

Ready! Set! Flip! This is where the action starts.

5. Note opponent's Battle Type. Compare Digimon Power.

If the game ended here, there wouldn't be much to it. You'd slap down a card, your opponent would slap down a card, and that would be the end of it. For instance, let's say you played the Rookie Agumon, and your opponent played the Rookie Candlemon.

As you can see, Agumon delivers 230 Power units against a Green Battle Type like Candlemon. Candlemon delivers 320 Power units against a Red Battle Type like Agumon. End of story? Nope. Read on!

6. Place Champion with correct Digivolve Requirements facedown on Digivolve Zone.

Easier said than done, right? Look through the ten cards you chose at random in step three. Hopefully, one of them will make your Digimon Digivolve to the next level.

How can you tell? Check out the names in the Digivolve Requirements Box. For instance, if you played your Rookie Agumon, and you have a Greymon or Rockmon in your group of ten, you're in business.

If you don't have any cards that can Digivolve your Rookie, you're out of luck. You will have to pass when you get to the next step of the game.

Digivolve

1. Flip a coin to see who goes first.

Penny, quarter, nickel, British pence. You get the picture.

2. First player turns over a card on Digivolve Zone, places it faceup on top of card on Duel Zone. Fulfill any requirements to complete turn.

If you've Digivolved from Rookie to Champion, you'll have to *Offline* one or two cards from the ten you chose in step three of Setup as payment, depending on what the card says.

If you're Digivolving from Champion to Ultimate or from Ultimate to Mega, you'll need to do one of two things:

• Put a Digivice Power Option card on the Power Port, or

• DNA Digivolve, which means you must play two lower-level cards instead of one. Stay tuned! More on this in the Power Option cards section, which follows.

There are a total of four Power Option cards that can be played during the Digivolve Phase. Two of them, the Digivice Power Option cards, we already mentioned. The other two are called Digivolve: To Champion and Digivolve: Ultra Digivolve. We talk about them more in the section of the book about Power Option cards.

3. Second player responds by Digivolving as above, or by saying, "Pass." If a player passes with a card facedown on Digivolve Zone, he or she must move it Offline. ("Use it, or lose it.")

If neither player can Digivolve, go on to Battle.

1. Take turns playing Power Option cards to Power Port, one card per turn, keeping track of changes in Digimon Power.

The player who went first during the last phase continues to go first.

Each Power Option card has an effect on your Digimon that usually increases its Power.

2. Continue until a player runs out of Options, or decides to stop, and says, "Pass." Other player may continue to play Power Option cards until he or she runs out or passes.

You might consider not using all of your Power Options if you don't need them to win. You'll definitely need them for later.

3. Compare Digimon Power to determine winner.

When play stops, the player showing the most Digimon Power wins the Duel.

4. Winner scores points based on Digivolve Level of loser, as shown in the Score section at bottom of winning card.

In other words, the higher your opponent's level, the more points you get for beating him or her.

Add your points to your Score Counter.

5. Winner keeps all Digimons on Duel Zone. Loser sends all Digimons, except Rookie, Offline. Offline all Power Option cards.

Both players send all Power Option cards Offline.

What if there's a tie? In that case, all Digimons remain on the Duel Zone and all Power Option cards are sent Offline. No points are scored. The winner of the previous Duel, or of the coin toss, goes first in the next Duel.

REGROUP

1. Restore hand to ten by drawing from Online deck. (You may first discard as many cards to Offline as you wish.)

If you aren't happy with the cards you're holding, this is your chance to try to get some better ones by discarding some and drawing from the top of the Online stack of cards.

2. When Online deck is down to zero, now or at *any time* during game, send *all* cards on your side of the board, except Rookie, Offline. Shuffle and return them facedown to Online. To regroup, draw as many as needed to restore your hand to ten cards.

3. You may change Rookie (place new Rookie facedown on old Rookie on Duel Zone), and you may place next-level Digimon facedown on Digivolve Zone.

If you weren't happy with the last Rookie you played, now is your chance to change your card. If you have a card with requirements to Digivolve one of the Rookies you hold in your hand, maybe you should give that Rookie a try.

4. Last winner starts new Duel by returning to Digivolve, step two.

Okay, so those are the basic rules. The next section of the book will talk about the Power Option cards and answer questions like "When should I change my Rookies?" and "Should I Digivolve from Champion to Ultimate instead?"

Let's go!

2

Power Option Cards

Power Option cards are where you get to turn your already-tough Digimon into a supermonster.

In all, there are three types of Power Option cards:

> Force FX cards (3)
> Digivolve cards (6)
> Power Blast cards (5)

for a total of fourteen in the Starter Set.

Most of the Power Option cards are used during the Battle Phase—but don't be fooled. There are five Digivolve cards that are used during the Digivolve Phase to pump your fighter up to the next level.

Here's an explanation of each Power Option card in the Starter Set.

Force FX Cards

Red, Yellow, & Green

Force FX Cards change the Digimon Power your Digimon delivers by switching the Battle Type it delivers no matter what your opponent's card says. Even if your opponent is Red, when you play the Yellow Force FX card, your Digimon delivers Power for the Yellow Battle Type.

Here's an example: Let's say Greymon goes up against Birdramon. Birdramon is a Green Battle Type, and Greymon normally delivers 340 Power points against Green.

Birdramon, by the way, delivers 410 Power points against Greymon's Red Battle Type, so at this point Greymon's in trouble.

But when you slap down a Yellow Force FX Power Option card, you automatically allow Greymon to use his Yellow Battle Type Power against Birdramon. Greymon fires a Nova Blast that pounds Birdramon with 420 points!

In the pages that follow, we list the Digimons whose power is strongest when each Force FX card is used.

These are usually the best times to use the card—but not the *only* time. You should always check your opponent's Power compared to yours to see if you should use a Force FX Card.

Note: The nice thing about Force FX cards is that they don't "cost" anything. You don't have to send any cards Offline to use them.

Red Offensive

This card changes your Digimon Power to Red, no matter what your opponent's color. This can be nice if you're stuck with a Digimon character whose other Battle Types are weaker than Red. But be careful! For some Digimons, Red is their weakest Battle Type, so you won't want to use this card for those Digimons.

Here's a list of Digimons whose Red Battle Type is the strongest:

Rookies

> Patamon
> Gotsumon
> Candlemon
> Gabumon

Champions

> Centarumon
> Starmon
> Wizardmon
> Coelamon
> Birdramon
> Garurumon

Ultimates

> Triceramon
> Piximon
> SkullMeramon

Mega

> SaberLeomon

Yellow Offensive

This card changes your Digimon Power to Yellow, no matter what your opponent's color.

Here's a list of Digimons whose Yellow Digimon Power is the strongest:

Rookies

> Gomamon
>
> Biyomon
>
> DemiDevimon
>
> Agumon
>
> Otamamon
>
> Kunemon
>
> Palmon
>
> Tentomon

Champions

> Apemon
>
> Greymon
>
> Dolphmon
>
> Tortomon
>
> Rockmon
>
> Musyamon
>
> (note: Green and Yellow are equal!)
>
> Dokugumon
>
> (note: Green and Yellow are equal!)

> Unimon
>
> Nanimon
>
> Angemon
>
> Ikkakumon
>
> Togemon
>
> Kabuterimon

Ultimates

> WereGarurumon
>
> Mammothmon
>
> Zudomon
>
> Okuwamon
>
> MegaKabuterimon

Mega

> HerculesKabuterimon

Green Offensive

This card changes your Digimon Power to Green, no matter what your opponent's color. Here's a list of Digimons whose Green Battle Type is the strongest:

Rookies

None

Champions

Musyamon
(note: Green and Yellow are equal!)
Dokugumon
(note: Green and Yellow are equal!)
Gekomon
Octomon
Bakemon

Ultimates

Kimeramon
SkullGreymon
MarineDevimon

Mega

Pukumon

Green Offensive Power Option cards affect the fewest Digimons— but some of those Ultimates pack a lot of Power!

Power Blast Cards

Blitz, Metal Attack, Counter Attack, Downgrade, Digi-Duel

Power Blast cards are used during the Battle Phase. They give you different advantages—but you have to pay a price. To use some of them, you have to send one, two, or even three cards Offline!

Blitz

This Power Blast card is your way of saying "Take that!" when you lose a round. If you play this card and lose the Digi-Duel, your opponent is still forced to send his top three Online cards to Offline.

Requirements: No cards

Metal Attack

This card packs a lot of punch! It adds 50 points to your Digimon Power.

Requirements: Send one card Offline.

Counter Attack

This card comes in handy when you're facing an opponent of a higher level. If you end up squaring off against someone higher on the food chain, use this card to double the number of your Digimon Power. This doubling lasts for the entire Duel.

Requirements: No cards Limitations: You *cannot* use this card with a Rookie.

Downgrade

This card lets you drop either your own Champion or your opponent's Champion to Rookie level. Put this card on the Power Port, and send either your Champion card or your opponent's Offline.

This card can help you against an opponent by weakening him. When he drops from Champion to Rookie, his Power level will drop.

You can also downgrade your *own* Digimon from Champion to Rookie. Why in the world would you want to do this? Don't you always want a Champion instead of a Rookie?

Not necessarily. Sometimes a Rookie might deliver more Power against a particular opponent, so it's actually an advantage to drop down to a lower level!

Requirements: Send one card Offline.

POWER OPTION   St-57
POWER BLAST

Downgrade

?

1st Edition

EFFECT: Downgrade either your Champion or your opponent's Champion to Rookie. Place this card on Power Port and send either your Champion or your opponent's Champion Offline. To use this card, send one card from your hand Offline.

•This effect applies to any player's Digimon.

© Akiyoshi Hongo • Toei Animation   © 1999 BANDAI

Digi-Duel

This card doesn't affect the actual Battle Phase at all. But if you feel like you're going to win the Duel, play this card and you'll *double* your score.

Requirements: Pretty hefty—Send three cards OFFLINE!

Digivolve Cards

To Champion, Ultra Digivolve, Digivice Red, Digivice Yellow, Digivice Green & Yellow, Digivice Red & Green

These cards are unlike the other Power Option cards because they are played during the Digivolve Phase. Use them to pump up your Digimon no matter what other requirements are needed!

Two of the cards, Digivolve To Champion and Ultra Digivolve, are special cards that allow you to bend the rules a bit.

The other four cards, called Digivice cards, are the cards that allow you to Digivolve into an Ultimate or Mega.

Digivolve To Champion

This card allows you to downgrade your Ultimate or Mega to Champion level.

Why downgrade? As we said earlier, sometimes downgrading actually gives your particular Digimon more Power against an opponent. Always remember, it's not just how high a level you reach, it's how much Power your Digimon can deliver!

Requirements: No cards

EFFECT: Downgrade your Ultimate or Mega to Champion. Place this card face down on Power Port and place Champion from your hand face down on Digivolve Zone.

•Use this card only during Digivolve Phase.

© Akiyoshi Hongo • Toei Animation   © 1999 BANDAI

EFFECT: Digivolve any Digimon to next Level, regardless of Digivolve Requirements. Place this card face down on Power Port and place next-level Digimon face down on Digivolve Zone. To use this card, send the rest of your hand Offline.

•Use this card only during Digivolve Phase.

© Akiyoshi Hongo • Toei Animation   © 1999 BANDAI

Ultra Digivolve

Zzaaap! Just like that, your Rookie becomes a Champion, your Champion jumps up to Ultimate, or your Ultimate morphs into a powerful Mega.

Requirements: Ouch! Send the rest of your hand Offline.

33

Digivice Red

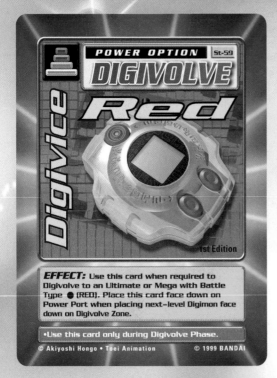

This card allows your Champion to Digivolve to Ultimate, or your Ultimate to Digivolve to Mega with a Red Battle Type. Unless you have one of the other special Digivolve cards, you must have one of these to get your Digimon to the higher levels.

Digivice Yellow

This card allows your Champion to Digivolve to Ultimate, or your Ultimate to Digivolve to Mega with a Yellow Battle Type. Unless you have one of the other special Digivolve cards, you must have one of these to get your Digimon to the higher levels.

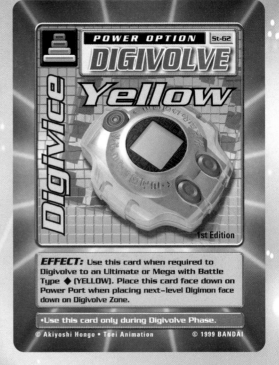

Digivice Red & Green

This card allows your Champion to Digivolve to Ultimate, or your Ultimate to Digivolve to Mega of either Red or Green Battle Types. Unless you have one of the other special Digivolve cards, you must have one of these to get your Digimon to the higher levels.

Digivice Green & Yellow

This card allows your Champion to Digivolve to Ultimate, or your Ultimate to Digivolve to Mega of either Yellow or Green Battle Types. Unless you have one of the other special Digivolve cards, you must have one of these to get your Digimon to the higher levels.

Quick Reference Guide

We've included this section to help you figure out just where your Digimons are headed as you try to help them Digivolve.

The whole point of Digivolving is to help your monster get stronger, but if he can't Digivolve into something powerful enough to trounce the other guy, what's the point?

The ways Digimons Digivolve can make you dizzy, so we've kept it pretty simple. We start with the Rookies, since that's where you start at the beginning of each Digi-Duel.

From there, we show you all the Champions that Rookies could Digivolve into.

Then, from the Champions, we show you all the Ultimates those Champions could become. Look closely! A few Champions are tough, but they don't Digivolve any higher.

Finally, we show you which Ultimates can Digivolve into Megas. Only a few Champions get that far, and you'll want to target those for maximum firepower.

Each page ends up looking sort of like a family tree, starting with the Rookie and spreading out. Each "branch" of the tree shows a possible way the creature could Digivolve.

By the way, we also show you how many cards you have to Offline in order to transform your Rookie into a Champion. We also show you what you need to get your Champion to jump up to Ultimate level, as well as Mega.

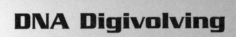

DNA Digivolving

You'll see many Digimons in here that "DNA Digivolve." That means that instead of Digivolving with a Digivice, they jump to the next level by combining with another Digimon—which means you need both cards.

A few Digimons require DNA Digivolving with Digimons that aren't included in the Starter Sets. We've still listed them here so that you'll be ready when the Booster Sets come out.

If you check through these "family trees," you should be able to create a good Battle Deck. The trees tell you how to get your Rookie up to Ultimate or even Mega level, and will also tell you what Digivices you'll need along the way!

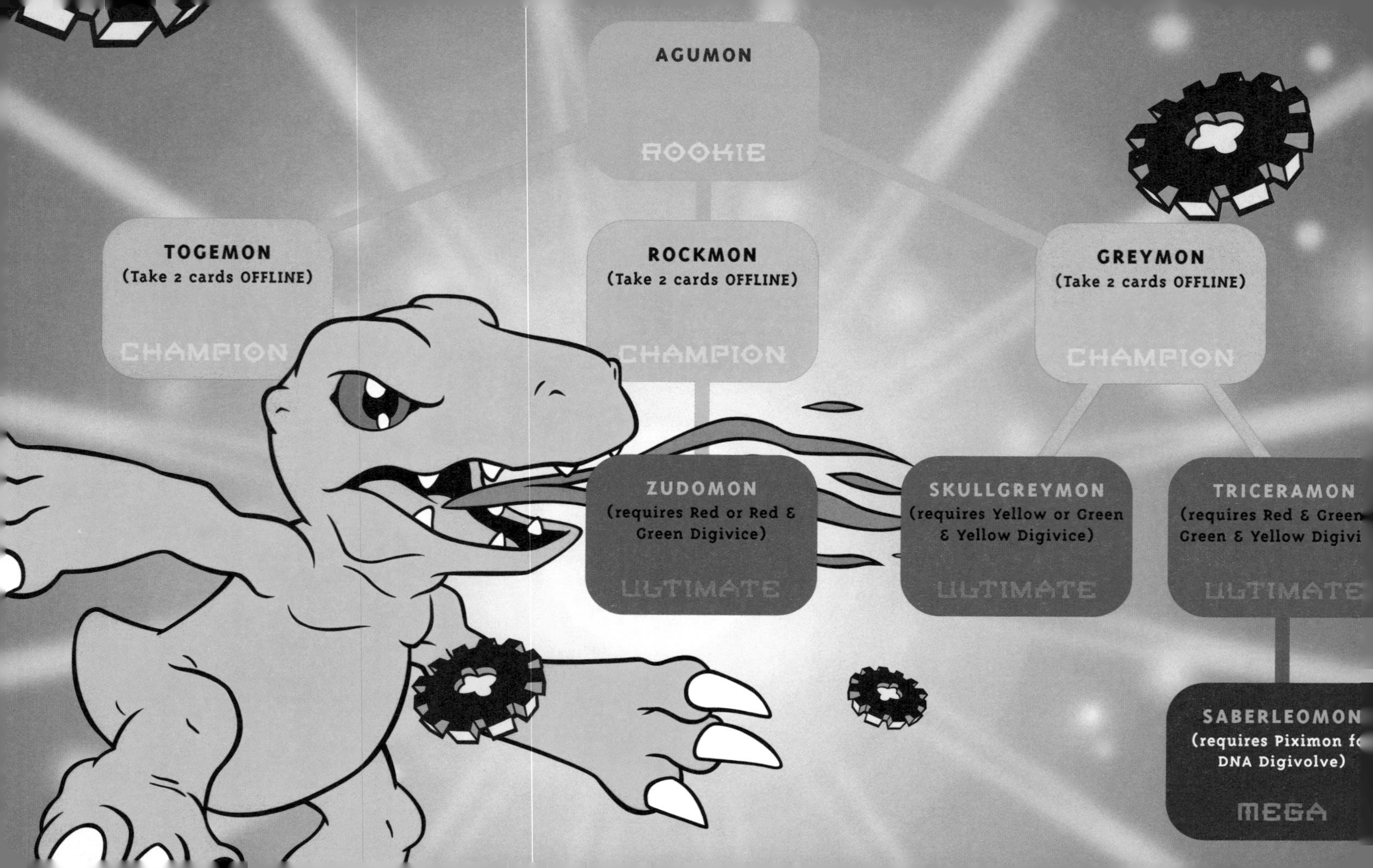

TOGEMON
(Take 2 cards OFFLINE)

CHAMPION

AGUMON

ROOKIE

ROCKMON
(Take 2 cards OFFLINE)

CHAMPION

ZUDOMON
(requires Red or Red &
Green Digivice)

ULTIMATE

SKULLGREYMON
(requires Yellow or Green
& Yellow Digivice)

ULTIMATE

GREYMON
(Take 2 cards OFFLINE)

CHAMPION

TRICERAMON
(requires Red & Green
Green & Yellow Digivi

ULTIMATE

SABERLEOMON
(requires Piximon fo
DNA Digivolve)

MEGA

BIYOMON

ROOKIE

BIRDRAMON
(Take 1 card OFFLINE)

CHAMPION

ROCKMON
(Take 2 cards OFFLINE)

CHAMPION

DOKUGUMON
(Take 2 cards OFFLINE)

CHAMPION

NANIMON
(Take 1 card OFFLINE)

CHAMPION

SKULLGREYMO
(requires Yellow or G__
& Yellow Digivice)

ULTIMATE

MEGAKABUTERIMON
(requires Red or Red &
Green Digivice)

ULTIMATE

PIXIMON
(requires Dokugumon for
DNA Digivolve)

ULTIMATE

PIXIMON
(requires Rockmon for
DNA Digivolve)

ULTIMATE

KIMERAMON
(requires Red & Green or
Green & Yellow Digivice)

ULTIMATE

**HERCULES-
KABUTERIMON**
(requires Red or Red &
Green Digivice)

MEGA

SABERLEOMON
(requires Triceramon for
DNA Digivolve)

MEGA

SABERLEOMON
(requires Triceramon for
DNA Digivolve)

MEGA

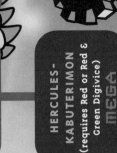

GABUMON
ROOKIE

GARURUMON
(Take 2 cards OFFLINE)
CHAMPION

ANGEMON
(Take 1 card OFFLINE)
CHAMPION

KABUTERIMON
(Take 2 cards OFFLINE)
CHAMPION

MAMMOTHMON
(requires Red or Red &
Green Digivice)
ULTIMATE

SKULLMERAMON
(requires Red & Green or
Green & Yellow Digivice)
ULTIMATE

SKULLGREYMON
(requires Yellow or Green
& Yellow Digivice)
ULTIMATE

MEGAKABUTERIMON
(requires Red or Red &
Green Digivice)
ULTIMATE

**HERCULES-
KABUTERIMON**
(requires Red or Red &
Green Digivice)
MEGA

TENTOMON
ROOKIE

KABUTERIMON
(Take 2 cards OFFLINE)
CHAMPION

TORTOMON
(Take 1 card OFFLINE)
CHAMPION

GEKOMON
(Take 1 card OFFLINE)
CHAMPION

SKULLGREYMON
(requires Yellow or Green & Yellow Digivice)
ULTIMATE

MEGAKABUTERIMON
(requires Red or Red & Green Digivice)
ULTIMATE

PIXIMON
(requires Gekomon for DNA Digivolve)
ULTIMATE

OKUWAMON
(requires Yellow or Green & Yellow Digivice)
ULTIMATE

PIXIMON
(requires Tortom DNA Digivolv)
ULTIMATE

KABUTERIMON
(res Red or Red & een Digivice)
TIMATE

HERCULES-KABUTERIMON
(requires Red or Red & Green Digivice)
MEGA

SABERLEOMON
(requires Triceramon for DNA Digivolve)
MEGA

HERCULES-KABUTERIMON
(requires Red or Red & Green Digivice)
MEGA

SABERLEOM
(requires Triceram DNA Digivolv)
MEGA

HERCULES-KABUTERIMON
(requires Red or Red & Green Digivice)
MEGA

CULES-UTERIMON
(res Red or Red & en Digivice)
MEGA

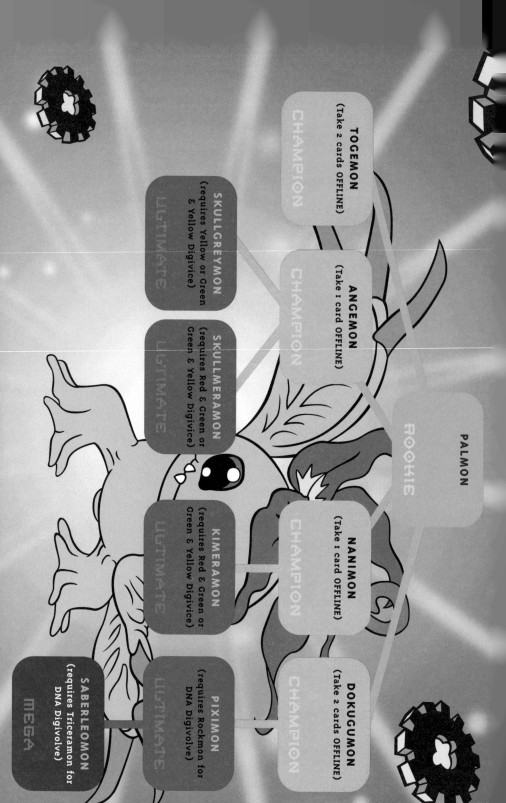

ROOKIE

PALMON

CHAMPION

TOGEMON
(Take 2 cards OFFLINE)

CHAMPION

ANGEMON
(Take 1 card OFFLINE)

CHAMPION

NANIMON
(Take 1 card OFFLINE)

CHAMPION

DOKUGUMON
(Take 2 cards OFFLINE)

ULTIMATE

SKULLGREYMON
(requires Yellow or Green
& Yellow Digivice)

ULTIMATE

SKULLMERAMON
(requires Red & Green or
Green & Yellow Digivice)

ULTIMATE

KIMERAMON
(requires Red & Green or
Green & Yellow Digivice)

ULTIMATE

PIXIMON
(requires Rockmon for
DNA Digivolve)

MEGA

SABERLEOMON
(requires Triceramon for
DNA Digivolve)

GOMAMON

ROOKIE

OCTOMON
(Take 2 cards OFFLINE)

CHAMPION

COELAMON
(Take 2 cards OFFLINE)

CHAMPION

DOLPHMON
(Take 1 card OFFLINE)

CHAMPION

IKKAKUMON
(Take 1 card OFFLINE)

CHAMPION

MARINEDEVIMON
(requires Yellow or Green
& Yellow Digivice)

ULTIMATE

ZUDOMON
(requires Red or Red &
Green Digivice)

ULTIMATE

ZUDOMON
(requires Red or Red &
Green Digivice)

ULTIMATE

PUKUMON
(requires any other
Ultimate for DNA Digivolve)

MEGA

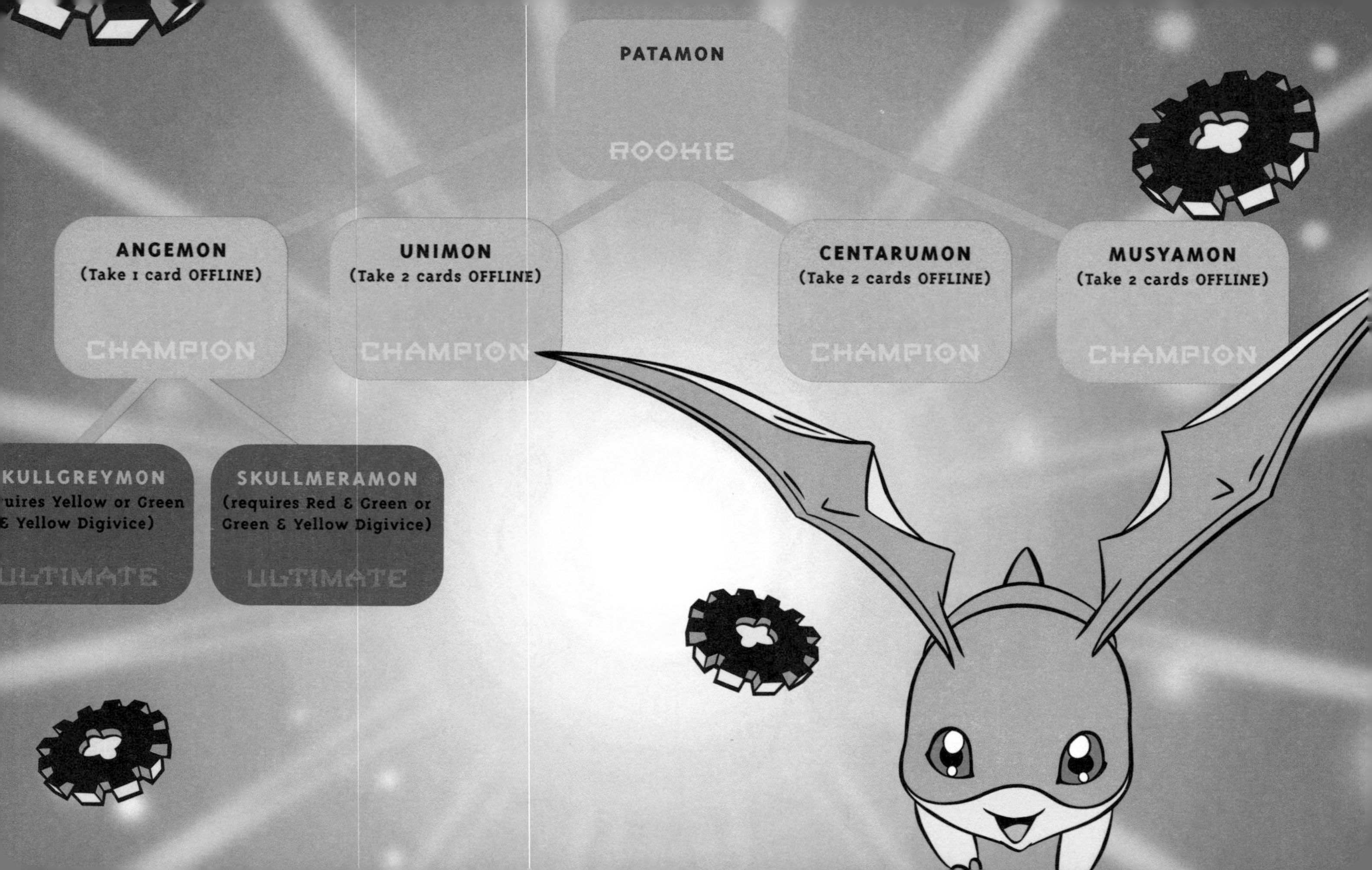

ULTIMATE

KULLGREYMON
uires Yellow or Green
e Yellow Digivice)

ULTIMATE

SKULLMERAMON
(requires Red & Green or
Green & Yellow Digivice)

CHAMPION

ANGEMON
(Take 1 card OFFLINE)

CHAMPION

UNIMON
(Take 2 cards OFFLINE)

ROOKIE

PATAMON

CHAMPION

CENTARUMON
(Take 2 cards OFFLINE)

CHAMPION

MUSYAMON
(Take 2 cards OFFLINE)

KUNEMON

ROOKIE

MUSYAMON
(Take 2 cards OFFLINE)

CHAMPION

ROOKIE

GOTSUMON

CHAMPION

TORTOMON
(Take 1 card OFFLINE)

STARMON
(Take 2 cards OFFLINE)

CHAMPION

GEKOMON
(Take 2 cards OFFLINE)

CHAMPION

ULTIMATE

KABUTERIMON
...ires Red or Red &
...reen Digivice)

ULTIMATE

PIXIMON
(requires Gekomon for
DNA Digivolve)

ULTIMATE

PIXIMON
(requires Monochromon
for DNA Digivolve)
MONOCHROMON WILL BE
INCLUDED IN LATER BOOSTER

ULTIMATE

TRICERAMON
(requires Red & Green or
Green & Yellow Digivice)

ULTIMATE

PIXIMON
(requires Tortomon for
DNA Digivolve)

ULTIMATE

OKUWAMO
(requires Yellow or R
& Yellow Digivi...)

ULTIMAT

**HERCULES-
KABUTERIMO...**
(requires Red or R...
Green Digivice)

MEGA

**HERCULES-
KABUTERIMON**
(...ires Red or Red &
...reen Digivice)

MEGA

SABERLEOMON
(requires Triceramon for
DNA Digivolve)

MEGA

SABERLEOMON
(requires Triceramon for
DNA Digivolve)

MEGA

SABERLEOMON
(requires Triceramon for
DNA Digivolve)

MEGA

SABERLEOMON
(requires Piximon for
DNA Digivolve)

MEGA

SABERLEOMON
(requires Triceramon for
DNA Digivolve)

MEGA

SABERLEOMON
(requires Triceramon for
DNA Digivolve)

OTAMAMON
ROOKIE

GEKOMON
(Take 1 card OFFLINE)
CHAMPION

STARMON
(Take 2 cards OFFLINE)
CHAMPION

TORTOMON
(Take 2 cards OFFLINE)
CHAMPION

OKUWAMO
(requires Yellow or
& Yellow Digivi
ULTIMATE

PIXIMON
(requires Tortomon for
DNA Digivolve)
ULTIMATE

TRICERAMON
(requires Red & Green or
Green & Yellow Digivice)
ULTIMATE

PIXIMON
(requires Monochromon
for DNA Digivolve)
MONOCHROMON WILL BE
INCLUDED IN LATER BOOSTER
ULTIMATE

PIXIMON
(requires Gekomon for
DNA Digivolve)
ULTIMATE

KABUTERIMON
ires Red or Red &
een Digivice)
ULTIMATE

HERCULES
KABUTERIM
(requires Red
Red & Green Digi
MEGA

SABERLEOMON
(requires Triceramon
for DNA Digivolve)
MEGA

SABERLEOMON
(requires Piximon
for DNA Digivolve)
MEGA

SABERLEOMON
(requires Triceramon
for DNA Digivolve)
MEGA

SABERLEOMON
(requires Triceramon for
DNA Digivolve)
MEGA

ERCULES-
BUTERIMON
ires Red or Red &
een Digivice)
MEGA

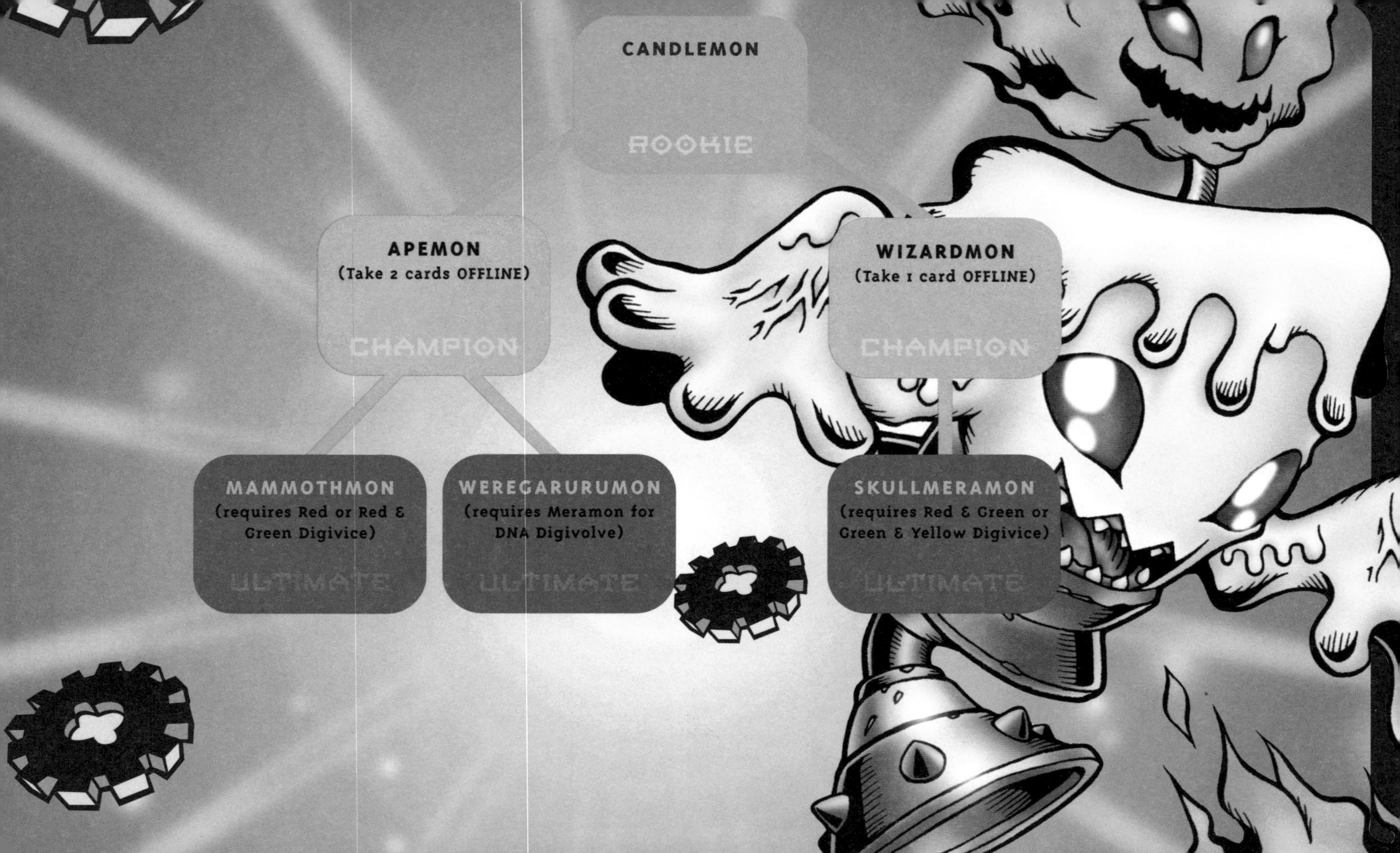

MAMMOTHMON
(requires Red or Red &
Green Digivice)

ULTIMATE

APEMON
(Take 2 cards OFFLINE)

CHAMPION

WEREGARURUMON
(requires Meramon for
DNA Digivolve)

ULTIMATE

CANDLEMON

ROOKIE

SKULLMERAMON
(requires Red & Green or
Green & Yellow Digivice)

ULTIMATE

WIZARDMON
(Take 1 card OFFLINE)

CHAMPION

DEMIDEVIMON

ROOKIE

BAKEMON
(Take 1 card OFFLINE)

CHAMPION

WIZARDMON
(Take 1 card OFFLINE)

CHAMPION

SKULLMERAMON
(requires Red & Green or
Green & Yellow Digivice)

ULTIMATE

WEREGARURUMON
(requires Garurumon for
DNA Digivolve)

ULTIMATE

4

Game Cards

Battle Decks

There are three ways to set up a Digimon Digi-Battle.

The first way is to lay out all the cards you have and take turns picking them until you each have a Battle Deck of thirty (then you put the last two cards away). The second is to follow a recommended pattern provided in the package. The third is to show up with your own premade Battle Deck. In each case, let's find the best way to get the strongest Battle Deck.

Pick and Choose

Okay, so all sixty-two cards are laid out in front of you. First things first—you have to decide who goes first. Usually, you can flip a coin.

Once it's your turn, you need to start building a "Digi-tree" of Digimons that will take you from Rookie to Mega. However, your choices need to be good, because your opponent is going to be picking cards, too!

The Digimon rules point out one way to choose your "Digi-tree." They say to start by picking Mega and work your way backward to Rookie. This is a good way to make sure you get what you want in the end.

But there's also another method. Use the Quick Reference Guide to find a Rookie who can Digivolve into the most Champions, Ultimates, and Megas, and pick that Rookie. That way, even if your opponent picks one of your possible levels, you have others.

Here's an example:

The Rookie Otamamon can Digivolve into three different Champions. Each of those Champions can Digivolve into two different Ultimates, and each Ultimate can Digivolve into a Mega. This makes Otamamon a good choice.

But watch out! Be sure you know all the requirements your Digimon needs. If you choose Otamamon and you want him to Digivolve to the Champion Gekomon and then to the Ultimate Piximon, you will also need the Champion Tortomon to get him there.

On the other hand, if you want Gekomon to Digivolve into the Champion Kuwagamon, all you need is the Yellow or Green & Yellow Digivice.

Patamon Digivolves into four pretty cool Champions (Angemon, Unimon, Centarumon, and Musyamon), but out of those four, only Angemon can Digivolve to an Ultimate.

If you choose wisely, you can end up with two or three Rookies, each with a couple of Champions, Ultimates, and Megas attached, and only take up about eighteen cards. This will leave you plenty of room left to include all the Power Option cards and Digivolve cards you need.

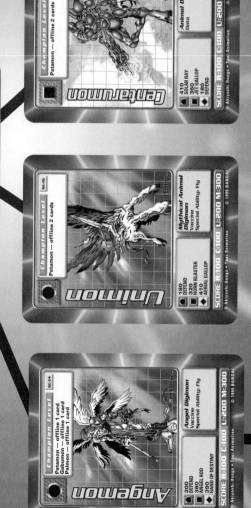

54

Digi-Tricks

If you're going to assemble your Battle Deck by the pick-and-choose method, here's a little secret that'll keep your opponent on his toes:

They say wars are won or lost before the battle's even fought. That may be true in the DigiWorld, too. Pay attention to the cards your opponent picks. It might be possible to weaken his Battle Deck just by choosing cards he or she needs. For instance, let's say he chooses the Rookie Agumon (he's a pretty popular Digimon). Now, Agumon can Digivolve into some pretty tough Champions and Ultimates, but you might notice that he can only reach one Mega: SaberLeomon. So if you see him select Agumon, you can nab SaberLeomon and keep him from ever getting to Mega level. It's sneaky but the game is all about strategy.

Using the Preconstructed Battle Deck

In the Digi-Battle game, you'll find a small card. On one side of the card is a list marked "Battle Deck—Hand #1." The other side is marked "Battle Deck—Hand #2."

These two hands are based on the Starter Set provided in the package. The Digimons are designed to help you advance from Rookie to Mega as long as you make good choices during the game itself.

Since there are sixty-two cards in the Starter Set, and only sixty are used during the game (thirty each), you'll have to discard two.

For this preconstructed Battle Deck, Kunemon and Pukumon have been left out.

Building Your Personal Battle Deck

Building your own deck is easier, because you don't have to worry about the other player nabbing your cards. Just be sure that you pay attention to the "Digi-tree" that will take your Rookie all the way to Mega.

As a general strategy, you can try to avoid Rookies who aren't going anywhere. Kunemon, for instance, only Digivolves into Musyamon, and Musyamon doesn't Digivolve any higher.

Sample Play

This section gives an example of how to play at the various stages of the game. If you're a beginner, you'll want to read this section. If you're not a beginner, what are you doing here? Go play!

Example: Otamamon v. Patamon

Digivolve Strategies and Power Option Cards

Let's say you and your opponent have already set up your Battle Decks and chosen your Rookies. You both turn your cards over to start the Digivolve Phase. You chose Otamamon, and you find yourself facing Patamon.

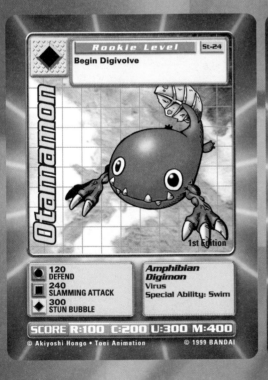

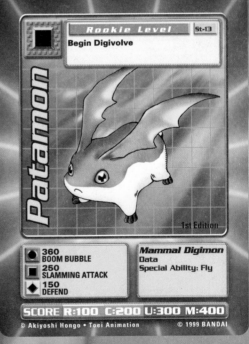

It's a good thing the game doesn't end here, because Patamon would end up as bait for Otamamon, who can deliver 240 Power points against Green, while Patamon can get only 150 points in defense.

But now you get to Digivolve. You've chosen Starmon as your Champion.

To get there, you have to Offline two cards. Here comes the strategy! Try not to Offline cards that you don't think you'll need. For instance, if you have a Yellow Offensive Card, you probably won't want it for Starmon, since his Yellow Power points aren't that strong.

Your opponent Digivolves into Angemon. Your Starmon delivers a powerful Meteor Stream at Angemon that's worth 460 points, while Angemon can only return 360 points with his Angel Rod. You're ready to rock and roll!

Battle Phase

But the fight's not over till the last card's dealt. During the Battle Phase, lots of things can happen. If your opponent won the coin toss, s/he goes first. If s/he has a Yellow Offensive Power Option card, s/he might use it to boost Angemon's Power up to 390.

If that happens, what should you do?

Pass.

I know passing isn't that exciting, but why not? You're still beating Angemon with 460 to your opponent's 390, and playing another card would only waste it. So just hold off and wait to see what happens.

At this point, you've got the Duel pretty much locked. Starmon's Meteor Stream is devastasting. Even if your opponent has a Metal Attack Power Option card, it's not going to pump him up enough to win. There's only one card you have to worry about: the Downgrade Power Option card.

This one can knock you back to a Rookie and, to make matters worse, Starmon has to Offline until you reshuffle the whole deck.

But if your opponent doesn't have the Downgrade Power Option card, you're in business!

Patamon Powwow

Okay, let's look at the same matchup from the other side. Pretend you're the one with Patamon, and you just lost to the Otamamon-to-Starmon Digivolution. Is there any way Patamon can come out on top? Should you take the first chance to replace poor little Patamon?

Not necessarily. Patamon can Digivolve into the Champions Angemon (as we saw), Unimon, Centarumon, and Musyamon. Unimon would suffer the same fate as Angemon, since they're both Red Types. But look at Centarumon and Musyamon. Although they don't deliver huge amounts of Power, Starmon doesn't pack such a wallop against them, either!

Against Centarumon's Green Type, Starmon delivers only 360 (remember, he delivered a devastasting 460 against Angemon).

Against Musyamon's Yellow Type, Starmon can fire off only a wimpy 200 points of Power.

Digi-Decisions, Decisions

The Digimon Digi-Battle card game is a game of give-and-take—which means that every time you give the other guy a good shot, you may take one next time!

That is the case in the example on the previous page. You might be able to use Musyamon to defeat Starmon—but then look at Musyamon himself. He can't really Digivolve any higher, and so while he defeats Starmon, he might end up on the losing end when your opponent brings on a stronger Champion and then Digivolves him to Ultimate.

Example: Facing a Higher-Level Opponent

Let's say that you've just lost a round. For the sake of the example, let's say your Ikkakumon just lost to Greymon.

Greymon stays on the Digi-board, but your Ikkakumon gets kicked off and you have to start again with the Rookie Comamon.

...ere's the problem. During ...e Digivolve Phase you ...n automatically upgrade ...omamon to another ...ampion—let's say this ...me you try Octomon ...ho's a better choice, ...ce he can get you to ...ega level).

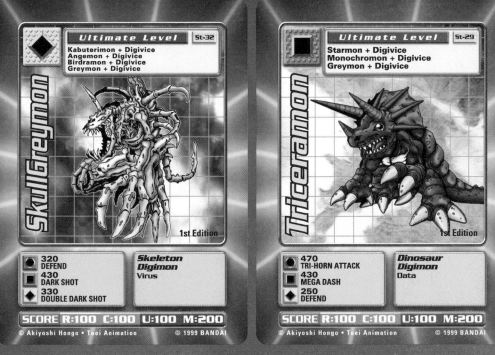

SkullGreymon

Ultimate Level | St-32

Kabuterimon + Digivice
Angemon + Digivice
Birdramon + Digivice
Greymon + Digivice

1st Edition

320 DEFEND
430 DARK SHOT
330 DOUBLE DARK SHOT

Skeleton Digimon
Virus

SCORE R:100 C:100 U:100 M:200

© Akiyoshi Hongo • Toei Animation   © 1999 BANDAI

Triceramon

Ultimate Level | St-29

Starmon + Digivice
Monochromon + Digivice
Greymon + Digivice

1st Edition

470 TRI-HORN ATTACK
430 MEGA DASH
250 DEFEND

Dinosaur Digimon
Data

SCORE R:100 C:100 U:100 M:200

© Akiyoshi Hongo • Toei Animation   © 1999 BANDAI

But your opponent can Digivolve too, which means your Octomon is going to face SkullGreymon or Triceramon.

Is there any hope? Can a Champion beat an Ultimate?

Of course! Let's say you Digivolve to Octomon and your opponent Digivolves to Triceramon. Check out the cards! Champion Octomon is pretty slick, and uses his Spurting Ink for 390 points against Triceramon's Green Type. Triceramon, even though he's an Ultimate, can only defend with 250 points against Octomon's Yellow Type.

Now, things can change once the Power Option cards come into play, but don't be afraid to put your Champion up against an Ultimate!

Remember, the best way to become a Digi-Battle expert is to learn the cards. Start trying to learn how each of your Digimons does against the Red, Green, and Yellow Power Types. Start knowing which Power Option cards will help your Digimons.

And also, start paying attention to the deck! Try to remember which Power Option cards have been used, which means they're Offline for at least a little while.

Good luck!

5

Story and Trading Cards

Collecting Digi-Mania!

Digimons! Digital Monsters!

The world of Digimons Digivolves from a handheld computer game to a TV show and now—trading cards!

But Digimon trading cards do more than just let you trade cards from the Digimon card game. Digimon trading cards bring the world of *Digimon: Digital Monsters*™ to life and let you learn even more about your favorite DigiWorld characters—the eight human characters, which you won't find in the game!

The Story of *Digimon: Digital Monsters*™

For a fifth-grade boy named Tai, one summer day at camp started out just like all the others. The sun was shining, the sky was clear, and Tai was taking a nap on the branch of a tree. Camp was fun enough, but slipping away from the day's activities to enjoy the outdoors was even better. Tai put his hands behind his head, closed his eyes, and sighed. "Ah, this is so cool."

Little did he know, it was about to get *much* cooler.

Without warning, the sky grew dark with clouds, and the air turned very cold. A moment later, Tai felt something cold touch his nose.

Tai swatted at his nose. "That felt like a snowflake . . . but it's summer!"

He looked up. More snowflakes swirled down from the sky. Tai stood up and jumped off the tree. Before he could take two steps the snow was coming down heavily. It was already starting to cover the ground.

Running toward the camp, Tai passed two other fifth graders, Sora and Matt.

"Hey, Matt!" he said to the boy. "What do you think of this weather?"

"Pretty flaky," Matt said.

Just then, a sixth grader named Joe appeared. He was also wondering where the snow had come from. Who wouldn't wonder? This was pretty strange cloud behavior for summer! The little group of curious kids grew. They were joined by a second grader named T.K., and two fourth graders named Izzy and Mimi.

The snow was beginning to reach blizzard proportions now, and a hard wind was throwing it right into their faces. "We should get back to camp!" Sora said.

"We'll never make it!" Tai said. The wind was blowing so loudly that they could barely hear one another.

And then, as quickly as it had started, the snow stopped.

"Thank goodness!" said Joe, who was frightened by almost anything. "Maybe things will get back to normal."

"Uh . . . I don't think so," said Tai. "Look!"

All seven kids looked up at the sky at once. A bright circle of light appeared out of nowhere—and it was growing fast.

Suddenly, seven streaks of light exploded from the circle and struck the ground at the kids' feet. They jumped back, startled. Luckily none of them had been hurt. But they were confused. A strange device floated before each kid. Slowly, Tai reached out and touched his. The others followed his lead.

And the world disappeared.

Tai felt like he was falling, falling, falling. He thought he must have gone a hundred miles down or more. Pretty spooky, right? He shouted in fear, but could barely hear his own voice. Just then, with a short *pop*, he stopped falling. He found himself lying on his back in the middle of a forest. Right on top of his chest was the strangest animal he had ever seen. It was small and round, with long ears, and it smiled down at him.

"Yah!" he yelled, jumping up and stumbling backward.

The little creature laughed. "Don't be afraid, Tai. I've been waiting for you! My name is Koromon."

Looking around, Tai realized that the other kids had all fallen into this forest with him. And each of them had been joined by an animal as strange and cute as Koromon.

"We're Digimons!" the animals said. "Digital Monsters!"

The Digimons patiently explained that the seven humans had landed on File Island in the Digital World.

"Oh, great," Tai said. "We're not just away from camp. We're not even on Earth!"

Before the Digimons could explain further, the seven kids and their newfound friends were attacked by a horrific monster shaped like a giant red beetle. "Kuwagamon!" the Digimons yelled. "Run!"

The kids sure didn't need to be told twice!

The giant red beetle zoomed close, trying to slice the kids with its Scissor Claws. Incredibly, the seven tiny Digimon creatures jumped between Kuwagamon and the humans. Fighting desperately, they managed to escape Kuwagamon's razor-sharp grasp.

But only for a moment.

Kuwagamon continued his attack, driving the children and the Digimons to the edge of a cliff. As brave as they were, the Digimons were too weak to defeat the mighty creature.

The kids had seen just about enough. Sure, Kuwagamon was scary, but who was he to attack seven little innocent Digimons? The kids were prepared to do anything to protect the tiny creatures . . . and then a miracle happened! Each of the kids felt something glowing on their belts, and realized that the strange devices they'd seen earlier were still with them. The devices burst into bright light, and that light appeared around the tiny Digimon.

The Digimons began to grow—to Digivolve—into more powerful creatures. Alone, they were still too weak to fight mighty Kuwagamon. But together with their new human friends, they became superstrong. They used their new powers to attack the huge monster. Finally, Kuwagamon was driven off.

Phew! The seven camp friends were safe for the moment. But they were also trapped in a strange new world full of unknown dangers. And they did not know how to get home.

They had escaped one monster, but their adventures were only beginning. . . .

The Characters in
Digimon: Digital Monsters™

Taichi Kamiya "Tai"

Tai is a fifth-grade boy and the natural-born leader of the kids caught in DigiWorld. Clever, confident, and a great athlete, Tai is an adventurer to the bone. His Digimon companion is Koromon, who Digivolves into the Rookie Agumon and the Champion Greymon.

Koromon

IN-TRAINING

Agumon

ROOKIE

Greymon

CHAMPION

69

Sora Takenouchi

Sora is a tomboy who loves to win. Like her friend Tai, she is a great athlete. Her Digimon friend is Yokomon, who Digivolves into the Rookie Biyomon and the Champion Birdramon.

Yokomon

IN-TRAINING

Biyomon

ROOKIE

Birdramon

CHAMPION

Yamato Ishida "Matt"

Matt is a cool kid with a soft spot for his kid brother, T.K. He didn't really know the others until they all got caught on File Island, but he quickly becomes their fast friend. His Digimon partner is Tsunomon, who Digivolves into the Rookie Gabumon and the Champion Garurumon.

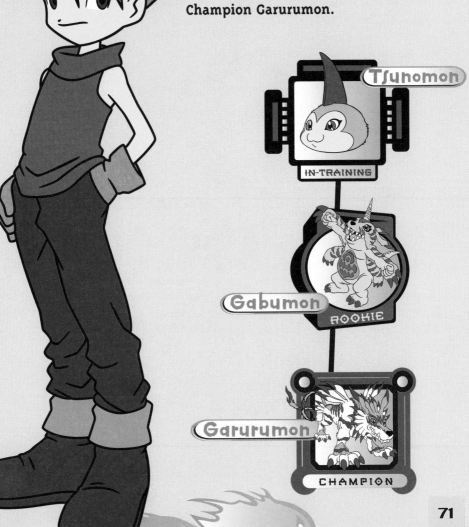

Tsunomon

IN-TRAINING

Gabumon

ROOKIE

Garurumon

CHAMPION

Koushirou Izumi "Izzy"

Izzy is a fourth grader who feels better tapping on his laptop computer than talking to another person. He's always polite to others, but he has trouble making friends because he spends more time gathering information than understanding his feelings. His Digimon companion is Motimon, who Digivolves into the Rookie Tentomon and the Champion Kabuterimon.

Motimon

IN-TRAINING

Tentomon

ROOKIE

Kabuterimon

CHAMPION

Mimi Tachikawa

Mimi is the prettiest girl in Izzy's class. She's also a little spoiled. In her world, she is used to getting everything she wants, and she finds DigiWorld to be quite a challenge. Her Digimon partner is Tanemon, who Digivolves into the Rookie Palmon and the Champion Togemon.

Tanemon

IN-TRAINING

Palmon

ROOKIE

Togemon

CHAMPION

Joe Kido

Joe is the oldest of the kids on File Island. He's also the best student. But that doesn't make him the best leader. So although he tries to guide them, he often finds himself the butt of their jokes. He always plays it safe, which isn't always the best way to survive in the world of Digimon! His Digimon friend is Bukamon, who Digivolves into the Rookie Gomamon and the Champion Ikkakumon.

Bukamon

IN-TRAINING

Gomamon

ROOKIE

Ikkakumon

CHAMPION

Takeru Takaishi "T.K."

T.K. is Matt's younger brother. Young and smart, he adapts easily to DigiWorld, but he doesn't like fighting and tries to avoid it whenever he can. His Digimon partner is Tokomon, who Digivolves into the Rookie Patamon and the Champion Angemon.

Tokomon

IN-TRAINING

Patamon

ROOKIE

Angemon

CHAMPION

Kari Kamiya

Kari is Tai's little sister. She's pretty fearless, especially for such a little kid, and is an adventurer like her brother. Her Digimon friend is Salamon, who Digivolves into the Champion Gatomon and the Ultimate Angewomon.

Salamon

ROOKIE

Gatomon

CHAMPION

Angewomon

ULTIMATE

Digimon Types

There are three types of Digimons: Vaccine, Virus, and Data.

Vaccine Digimons are good. They use their great strength only to help others and to defend themselves. However, some Vaccine Digimons have fallen under the control of Devimon's Black Gears, and fight for evil until they are released.

Virus Digimons are evil Digimons. They don't need any Black Gears to do their nastiest work. The worst of the Virus Digimons is Devimon, who sends his Black Gears to bend even good Digimons to his evil will.

Data Digimons are normally programmed Digimons. Their characteristics vary by evolution and environment. In other words, they can be good or evil depending on their Digivolution or what environment they are in.

A Note about the First Thirty-four Cards

The first three cards are special: They have no numbers. They show collections of the Digimon children, Digimon Rookies, and Digimon Champions. So even though there are thirty-four cards, only thirty-one of them are listed with a number on the bottom left corner.

The three special cards are listed first.

The list then starts with #1.

Seven children trapped in the world of Digimons. Will they have the courage and strength to find a way home?

With the help of the kids, the In-Training Digimons Digivolve to Rookies to fight off evil monsters!

Thanks to the Digivices and their own good hearts, the seven kids help transform their Digimon friends into Champions!

Digivolve! Champions!! DP 450

Champion Digimons

Digimon#
Digivolve Champions! 3 of 34

The Digivice is the key to Digivolving

Through friendship, teamwork, and honesty, the kids activate the Digivice to digivolve their Digimon pals.

DIGIMON

© Akiyoshi Hongo • Toei Animation. TM and © 1999 Bandai. The card/hologram combination is a trademark of The Upper Deck Company, LLC. © 2000 The Upper Deck Company, LLC. All Rights Reserved. Printed in the U.S.A.

Tai & Koromon
Together, they're an unbeatable team!

DIGIMON

1 Tai & Koromon DP 200

In-Training Digimon

Digimon #1
Koromon 4 of 34

IN-TRAINING DIGIMON

• Group: Micro Digimon
• Type: None
• Technique: Bubble-Blow
• Size: 10.0 G

Taichi "TAI" Kamiya
Tai is a natural leader. He is quick to make decisions and takes the initiative in all group events. He can be reckless.

DIGIMON

© Akiyoshi Hongo • Toei Animation. TM and © 1999 Bandai. The card/hologram combination is a trademark of The Upper Deck Company, LLC. © 2000 The Upper Deck Company, LLC. All Rights Reserved. Printed in the U.S.A.

Card 5 of 34

Matt & Tsunomon
Always ready to make a friend laugh or make evil creatures run!

Card 6 of 34

Sora & Yokomon
An unbeatably fierce team when Yokomon Digivolves to Biyomon.

Izzy & Motimon
Motimon keeps Izzy focused when danger is at hand.

Mimi & Tanemon
Tanemon helps Mimi adapt to the weird Digimon world.

Joe & Bukamon
Joe learns courage with Bukamon at his side.

Digimon #6
Bukamon

9 of 34

IN-TRAINING DIGIMON

- Group: Micro Digimon
- Type: None
- Technique: Bubble-Blow
- Size: 7.0 G

Joe Kido

Joe is a serious boy and a good student. Joe's immediate reaction to trouble is to run, but he always comes through when the group is in danger.

6 Joe & Bukamon DP 250

In-Training Digimon

T.K. & Tokomon
Power packed in a small package!

Digimon #7
Tokomon

10 of 34

IN-TRAINING DIGIMON

- Group: Micro Digimon
- Type: None
- Technique: Bubble-Blow
- Size: 10.0 G

Takeru "T.K." Takaishi

T.K. is Matt's younger brother. He is a sweet kid and everyone likes him. Even though he is the youngest, T.K. doesn't panic in a crisis.

7 T.K. & Tokomon DP 200

In-Training Digimon

Doubling in size from Koromon to Agumon, this Digimon packs a lot of Power into his Pepper Breath.

The Rookie Gabumon fights fiercely to protect his friend Matt.

The Rookie Biyomon looks pretty, but her Spiral Twister packs a lot of punch.

10 Biyomon DP 300

Rookie Digimon

Digimon #10
Biyomon 13 of 34

ROOKIE DIGIMON

- Group: Bird Digimon
- Type: Vaccine
- Technique: Spiral Twister
- Size: 15.0 G

Firing Spiral Twister!
Biyomon fires a Spiral Twister at her enemies to defeat them and protect Sora!

If any bad guys "bug" this insectoid, he'll let them know it!

11 Tentomon DP 200

Rookie Digimon

Digimon #11
Tentomon 14 of 34

ROOKIE DIGIMON

- Group: Insectoid Digimon
- Type: Vaccine
- Technique: Super Shocker
- Size: 15.0 G

Lightning Super Shocker!
Aimed at the enemy's weakness, Tentomon attacks with a Super Shocker.

Mimi can be a "shrinking violet," but the vegetation Digimon Palmon always helps her to bloom.

When Gomamon knows something's "fishy," he uses his Power to keep his friends safe.

Patamon is protective of everyone in the group, especially T.K.!

The children and their friends realize that defeating Kuwagamon's
Scissor Claw won't be a snap!

Greymon is one of the most powerful of the Digimons. It's a good thing he's on our side!

16 Greymon DP 420

Champion Digimon

Digimon #16 **Greymon** 19 of 34

CHAMPION DIGIMON

- Group: Dinosaur Digimon
- Type: Vaccine
- Technique: Nova Blast
- Size: 30.0 G

Nova Blast Power!
With a very powerful Nova Blast, Greymon defeats the enemy!

One strike of Garurumon's ear-shattering Howling Blaster sends the evil creatures controlled by the Black Gears running for cover!

18 Garurumon DP 300

Champion Digimon

Digimon #18 **Garurumon** 20 of 34

CHAMPION DIGIMON

- Group: Animal Digimon
- Type: Vaccine
- Technique: Howling Blaster
- Size: 20.0 G

Evil Seadramon Attack
Garurumon defends himself against Seadramon's attacks and defeats him with a powerful Howling Blaster.

Just when you thought it was safe to go back into the ocean! Seadramon is definitely not something you want to be on the bad side of.

A fierce Digimon, Monochromon is also incredibly strong.

And you thought thunder and lightning were powerful! Wait until you hear Birdramon fly by, and see the Power of his devastating Meteor Wing!

If you play with fire, you're sure to get burned. Meramon guards Mount Miharashi.

He may look nasty, but Kabuterimon is a Champion of good. When Virus Digimons challenge him they're in for quite a shock!

Armed with his Needle Spray, Togemon always gets his point across. But he has more weapons, too, including a knockout Power Punch.

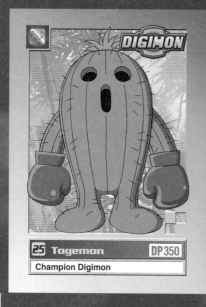

What do you do when you're faced with 25.0 G of fur and teeth? Be glad he's a Vaccine Digimon!

When the kids first met Leomon he was under the control of the Black Gears. Now he is as free as a wild animal—and twice as fierce!

Ready to join the club? Ogremon thinks it'd be a smash! This fierce fighter is almost enough to tame even the likes of Leomon!

Digimon #31
Ogremon

29 of 34

CHAMPION DIGIMON

- Group: Evil Digimon
- Type: Virus
- Finish Blow: Pummel Whack
- Size: 20.0 G

Pummel Whack!
Leomon tries to stop Devimon in his evil tracks! Ogremon helps Devimon attack Leomon with his Pummel Whack!

31 Ogremon   DP 380
Champion Digimon

Devimon controls the Black Gears that turn good Digimons into bad. If he is not stopped, he'll take over DigiWorld—and Earth as well!

Digimon #32
Devimon

30 of 34

CHAMPION DIGIMON

- Group: Evil Digimon
- Type: Virus
- Technique: Touch of Evil
- Size: 15.0 G

The Touch of Evil!
Devimon brainwashes good Digimon towards his evil ways with THE BLACK GEARS. He dominates File Island, then aspires to take over the world!

32 Devimon   DP 350
Champion Digimon

Cute and cuddly? Don't be fooled. Frigimon is one tough customer with the Power to knock evil Digimons cold!

Digimon #33
Frigimon

31 of 34

CHAMPION DIGIMON

● Group: Icy Digimon

● Type: Vaccine

● Technique: Subzero Ice Punch

● Size: 30.0 G

Subzero Ice Punch!
The kids free Frigimon from the grip of THE BLACK GEARS. To repay them for their kindness, Frigimon stays with the kids and helps them fight the evil Mojyamon.

33 Frigimon   DP 300

Champion Digimon

Bakemon may have less Digimon Power than the others, but he makes up for it in sheer fright.

Digimon #37
Bakemon

32 of 34

CHAMPION DIGIMON

● Group: Ghost Digimon

● Type: Virus

● Finish Blow: Dark Claw

● Size: 30.0 G

Ghost of a Chance!
Ghostly Bakemon tries to capture the kids when they wander into his cemetery! Joe foils Bakemon by reciting special verses!

37 Bakemon   DP 250

Champion Digimon

When the kids feel like they're flying on a wing and a prayer, Angemon is there to help them.

Digimon #43
Angemon

33 of 34

CHAMPION DIGIMON

- Group: Angel Digimon
- Type: Vaccine
- Technique: Hand of Fate
- Size: 20.0 G

Hand of Fate!

In order to defeat the gigantic Devimon, Patamon digivolves to Angemon, who uses his powerful Hand of Fate to extinguish Devimon.

43 Angemon   DP 380

Champion Digimon

Kokatorimon's Power is enough to make anyone chicken! His Frozen Fire Shot can turn even a Rookie as tough as Agumon to stone.

Digimon #50
Kokatorimon

34 of 34

CHAMPION DIGIMON

- Group: Bird Digimon
- Type: Data
- Finish Blow: Frozen Fire Shot
- Size: 20.0 G

Stone Cold!

Kokatorimon shoots his Frozen Fire Shot at Agumon and turns him to stone! When Agumon is frozen, Kokatorimon steals the Crest tags!

50 Kokatorimon   DP 280

Champion Digimon

And now for something really special. . . . There are nine more cool Digimon cards to trade and collect. Check these out!

Card U1 of U8

Andromon is a superstrong Digimon who lives in a factory that assembles machines only to take them apart again.

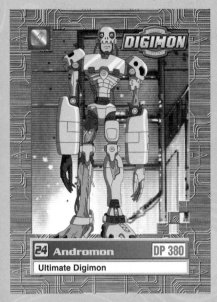

Digimon #24
Andromon

ULTIMATE DIGIMON

- Group: Android Digimon
- Type: Vaccine
- Technique: Lightning Blade
- Size: 25.0 G

Lightning Blade!

The kids rescued Andromon, who was stuck in a machine. But they didn't know he was controlled by THE BLACK GEARS. He attacks them with the Lightning Blade.

24 Andromon   DP 380

Ultimate Digimon

Card U2 of U8

This giant teddy bear is infected by the Black Jewel. You definitely won't want to snuggle up with this big bear!

Digimon #27
Monzaemon

ULTIMATE DIGIMON

- Group: Puppet Digimon
- Type: Vaccine
- Technique: Hearts Attack
- Size: 40.0 G

Hearts Attack!

Monzaemon is controlled by THE BLACK JEWEL, and his good nature turns villainous. The evil power takes over and he strikes the kids with his Hearts Attack.

27 Monzaemon   DP 500

Ultimate Digimon

Etemon looks like one cool dude with his guitar and dark shades, but wear your earplugs if he's ever giving a concert!

Digimon #46
Etemon

U3 of 8

ULTIMATE DIGIMON

- Group: Puppet Digimon
- Type: Virus
- Technique: Dark Network & Concert Crush
- Size: 20.0 G

The Dark Network!
Etemon's special weapon is The Dark Network, that creates a black hole to suck the life out of everything!

46 Etemon   DP 500

Ultimate Digimon

Tai helped Greymon Digivolve to SkullGreymon, then this Skeleton Digimon turned on the good Digimons and even the kids.

Digimon #49
SkullGreymon

U4 of 8

ULTIMATE DIGIMON

- Group: Skeleton Digimon
- Type: Virus
- Finish Blow: Dark Shot
- Size: 40.0 G

Dark Shot!
Tai makes a mistake and accidentally digivolves Greymon to SkullGreymon, who is out of control! Fortunately, his Dark Shot destroys the evil Digimon!

49 SkullGreymon   DP 400

Ultimate Digimon

She may be tiny, but Piximon turns out to be very necessary to the kids' survival. She is the Digimon who trains the kids for battle.

MetalGreymon Digivolves from Greymon to save the kids from Etemon's evil Black energy.

WereGarurumon is not only an Ultimate Digimon, he's also the ultimate protector of Matt and his friends. Howl!!

Digimon #56
WereGarurumon

U7 of 8

ULTIMATE
DIGIMON

- Group: Animal Digimon
- Type: Vaccine
- Finish Blow: Wolf Claw
- Size: 18.0 G

Wolf Claw!

Matt and Joe get caught by Digitamamon! Matt's Crest of Friendship comes to life causing Garurumon to digivolve to the Ultimate WereGarurumon. WereGarurumon blows Digitamamon away with his Wolf Claw!

56 WereGarurumon DP 350

Ultimate Digimon

When the kids get into hot water, MegaKabuterimon is on the scene to "bug" their opponents until they leave the kids alone.

Digimon #87
MegaKabuterimon

U8 of 8

ULTIMATE
DIGIMON

- Group: Insectoid Digimon
- Type: Vaccine
- Finish Blow: Horn Buster
- Size: 30.0 G

Horn Buster!

Izzy temporarily loses his curiosity, due to the evil plan of Vademon, causing Tentomon to go back to his in training mode. When Izzy regains his curiosity, Tentomon digivolves to the Ultimate MegaKabuterimon! He knocks down Vademon with his Horn Buster!

87 MegaKabuterimon DP 400

Ultimate Digimon

This supercool, superspecial CD-ROM trading card comes with so many awesome features, it's hard to describe them all here. But we'll give it a try!

When you install this CD-ROM on your computer, the first thing you hear is the *Digimon: Digital Monsters™* television show theme song. You can sing along while you check out the whole CD-ROM, because the theme song never stops playing!

From the home page of the CD-ROM card, you can choose four different paths (besides Quit and Help, that is). The first is a **Digimon Video**, which shows all of your favorite Digimons Digivolving from their In-Training to their Rookie levels. Wow! Next, you can view the **Digimon Story**, which is kind of an introduction to the DigiDestined, their Digimons, and how they all found each other and adventure in DigiWorld. Of course, you can also click on **Links**. One link, which says Bandai®, takes you to www.foxkids.com, home page of *Digimon: Digital Monsters™*. The other link takes you to Upper Deck™, who made this awesome CD-ROM card. You definitely won't want to miss either of those links for the complete background on *Digimon: Digital Monsters™*. Finally, you can click on each of the seven human characters on the home page individually. For each character there is an introduction, what his or her best qualities are, who his or her Digimon bud is, and what s/he is known for. All this and awesome graphics that you can't find anywhere else! This CD-ROM trading card is a definite must-have for *Digimon: Digital Monsters™* fans!

Digi-Appendix

Digimon Digi-Battle Game Card Checklist

Check on these pages for a list of all of the Digimon character game cards that are currently available. Don't worry if you don't have them all yet. You can collect the ones you don't have by checking out the Digimon Booster Sets. Check them off as you get them. Have fun!

Starter Cards

Rookie Level	St-01
Begin Digivolve	

Agumon

140 DEFEND	*Reptile Digimon*
230 CLAW ATTACK	Vaccine
380 PEPPER BREATH	

SCORE **R:100 C:200 U:300 M:400**

© Akiyoshi Hongo • Toei Animation   © 1999 BANDAI

Champion Level	St-02
Agumon — offline 2 cards	

Greymon

1st Edition

220 DEFEND	*Dinosaur Digimon*
340 GREAT HORNS ATTACK	Vaccine
420 NOVA BLAST	

SCORE **R:100 C:100 U:200 M:300**

© Akiyoshi Hongo • Toei Animation   © 1999 BANDAI

☐ Agumon

☐ Greymon

Biyomon (St-03)

Rookie Level

Begin Digivolve

1st Edition

- ● 140 DEFEND
- ■ 240 PECKING ATTACK
- ◆ 350 SPIRAL TWISTER

Bird Digimon
Vaccine
Special Ability: Fly

SCORE R:100 C:200 U:300 M:400

© Akiyoshi Hongo • Toei Animation   © 1999 BANDAI

 Biyomon

Birdramon (St-04)

Champion Level

Biyomon — offline 1 card

1st Edition

- ● 410 METEOR WING
- ■ 360 FIRE FLAPPING
- ◆ 200 DEFEND

Bird Digimon
Data
Special Ability: Fly

SCORE R:100 C:100 U:200 M:300

© Akiyoshi Hongo • Toei Animation   © 1999 BANDAI

Birdramon

Gabumon (St-05)

Rookie Level

Begin Digivolve

1st Edition

- ● 350 BLUE BLASTER
- ■ 240 HORN ATTACK
- ◆ 150 DEFEND

Reptile Digimon
Data

SCORE R:100 C:200 U:300 M:400

© Akiyoshi Hongo • Toei Animation   © 1999 BANDAI

Gabumon

Garurumon (St-06)

Champion Level

Gabumon — offline 2 cards
Tapirmon — offline 1 card

1st Edition

- ● 410 HOWLING BLASTER
- ■ 330 SLAMMING ATTACK
- ◆ 180 DEFEND

Animal Digimon
Data

SCORE R:100 C:100 U:200 M:300

© Akiyoshi Hongo • Toei Animation   © 1999 BANDAI

 Garurumon

Tentomon

Rookie Level St-07

Begin Digivolve

1st Edition

- 100 DEFEND
- 250 TALON ATTACK
- 350 SUPER SHOCKER

Insectoid Digimon
Vaccine
Special Ability: Fly

SCORE R:100 C:200 U:300 M:400

© Akiyoshi Hongo • Toei Animation   © 1999 BANDAI

☐ Tentomon

Kabuterimon

Champion Level St-08

Tentomon — offline 2 cards
Gabumon — offline 2 cards

1st Edition

- 200 DEFEND
- 340 BEETLE HORN ATTACK
- 410 ELECTRO SHOCKER

Insectoid Digimon
Vaccine
Special Ability: Fly

SCORE R:100 C:100 U:200 M:300

© Akiyoshi Hongo • Toei Animation   © 1999 BANDAI

☐ Kabuterimon

Palmon

Rookie Level St-09

Begin Digivolve

1st Edition

- 130 DEFEND
- 250 STINKING ATTACK
- 370 POISON IVY

Vegetation Digimon
Data

SCORE R:100 C:200 U:300 M:400

© Akiyoshi Hongo • Toei Animation   © 1999 BANDAI

☐ Palmon

Togemon

Champion Level St-10

Palmon — offline 2 cards
Agumon — offline 2 cards

1st Edition

- 200 DEFEND
- 300 LIGHT SPEED JABBING
- 360 NEEDLE SPRAY

Vegetation Digimon
Virus

SCORE R:100 C:100 U:200 M:300

© Akiyoshi Hongo • Toei Animation   © 1999 BANDAI

☐ Togemon

Rookie Level St-11

Begin Digivolve

Gomamon

140 DEFEND
250 CLAW ATTACK
350 MARCHING FISHES

Sea Animal Digimon
Vaccine
Special Ability: Swim

SCORE **R:100 C:200 U:300 M:400**

© Akiyoshi Hongo • Toei Animation   © 1999 BANDAI

☐ Gomamon

Champion Level St-12

Gomamon — offline 1 card
Syakomon — offline 2 cards

Ikkakumon

210 DEFEND
360 HEAT TOP
370 HARPOON TORPEDO

Sea Animal Digimon
Vaccine
Special Ability: Swim

SCORE **R:100 C:100 U:200 M:300**

© Akiyoshi Hongo • Toei Animation   © 1999 BANDAI

☐ Ikkakumon

Rookie Level St-13

Begin Digivolve

Patamon

360 BOOM BUBBLE
250 SLAMMING ATTACK
150 DEFEND

Mammal Digimon
Data
Special Ability: Fly

SCORE **R:100 C:200 U:300 M:400**

© Akiyoshi Hongo • Toei Animation   © 1999 BANDAI

☐ Patamon

Champion Level St-14

Patamon — offline 1 card
Gabumon — offline 1 card
Palmon — offline 1 card

Angemon

200 DEFEND
360 ANGEL ROD
390 HAND OF DESTINY

Angel Digimon
Vaccine
Special Ability: Fly

SCORE **R:100 C:100 U:200 M:300**

© Akiyoshi Hongo • Toei Animation   © 1999 BANDAI

☐ Angemon

Nanimon

Champion Level St-15

Biyomon — offline 1 card
Palmon — offline 1 card

1st Edition

- 100 DEFEND
- 220 PUNCHER
- 300 POWER DRIVE

Invader Digimon
Virus
Special Effect: Send 1 card from opponent's Online to Offline when this Digimon wins.

SCORE R:100 C:200 U:300 M:400

© Akiyoshi Hongo • Toei Animation   © 1999 BANDAI

☐ **Nanimon**

Unimon

Champion Level St-16

Patamon — offline 2 cards

1st Edition

- 180 DEFEND
- 320 HORN BLASTER
- 410 AERIAL GALLOP

Mythical Animal Digimon
Vaccine
Special Ability: Fly

SCORE R:100 C:100 U:200 M:300

© Akiyoshi Hongo • Toei Animation   © 1999 BANDAI

☐ **Unimon**

Centarumon

Champion Level St-17

Patamon — offline 2 cards

1st Edition

- 410 SOLAR RAY
- 360 JET GALLOP
- 180 DEFEND

Animal Digimon
Data

SCORE R:100 C:100 U:200 M:300

© Akiyoshi Hongo • Toei Animation   © 1999 BANDAI

☐ **Centarumon**

Kunemon

Rookie Level St-18

Begin Digivolve

1st Edition

- 160 DEFEND
- 240 POISON WINDER
- 300 ELECTRO THREAD

Larva Digimon
Virus
Special Ability: Dig

SCORE R:100 C:200 U:300 M:400

© Akiyoshi Hongo • Toei Animation   © 1999 BANDAI

☐ **Kunemon**

Dokugumon

Champion Level St-19

Biyomon — offline 2 cards
Palmon — offline 2 cards

240 DEFEND
350 POISON COBWEB
350 POISON THREAD

Insectoid Digimon
Virus

SCORE R:100 C:100 U:200 M:300

Musyamon

Champion Level St-20

Patamon — offline 2 cards
Kunemon — offline 2 cards

290 DEFEND
350 NINJA BLADE
350 SHOGUN SWORD

Wizard Digimon
Virus

SCORE R:100 C:100 U:200 M:300

Kimeramon

Ultimate Level St-21

Nanimon + Digivice

480 SCISSOR CLAW
520 POISON WING
220 DEFEND

Composition Digimon
Data
Special Ability: Fly

SCORE R:100 C:100 U:100 M:200

Rockmon

Champion Level St-22

Agumon — offline 2 cards
Biyomon — offline 2 cards

230 DEFEND
300 ROCK BALL
380 ROCK PUNCH

Rock Digimon
Virus
Special Ability: Dig

SCORE R:100 C:100 U:200 M:300

Rookie Level — St-23
Begin Digivolve

Gotsumon

1st Edition

- ● 330 ROCK FIST
- ■ 250 CRAZY CRUSHER
- ◆ 100 DEFEND

Rock Digimon
Data
Special Ability: Dig

SCORE R:100 C:200 U:300 M:400

© Akiyoshi Hongo • Toei Animation   © 1999 BANDAI

☐ Gotsumon

Rookie Level — St-24
Begin Digivolve

Otamamon

1st Edition

- ● 120 DEFEND
- ■ 240 SLAMMING ATTACK
- ◆ 300 STUN BUBBLE

Amphibian Digimon
Virus
Special Ability: Swim

SCORE R:100 C:200 U:300 M:400

© Akiyoshi Hongo • Toei Animation   © 1999 BANDAI

☐ Otamamon

Champion Level — St-25
Tentomon — offline 1 card
Gotsumon — offline 1 card
Otamamon — offline 2 cards

Tortomon

1st Edition

- ● 210 DEFEND
- ■ 360 SPINNING ATTACK
- ◆ 370 STRONG CARAPACE

Reptile Digimon
Vaccine

SCORE R:100 C:100 U:200 M:300

© Akiyoshi Hongo • Toei Animation   © 1999 BANDAI

☐ Tortomon

Champion Level — St-26
Gotsumon — offline 2 cards
Otamamon — offline 2 cards

Starmon

1st Edition

- ● 460 METEOR STREAM
- ■ 350 HYPNOTISM
- ◆ 200 DEFEND

Mutant Digimon
Data

SCORE R:100 C:100 U:200 M:300

© Akiyoshi Hongo • Toei Animation   © 1999 BANDAI

☐ Starmon

Gekomon (St-27)

Champion Level — St-27

Tentomon — offline 1 card
Gotsumon — offline 2 cards
Otamamon — offline 1 card

1st Edition

- 270 DEFEND
- 390 SYMPHONY CRUSHER
- 380 TONGUE ATTACK

Amphibian Digimon
Virus

SCORE R:100 C:100 U:100 M:200

© Akiyoshi Hongo • Toei Animation   © 1999 BANDAI

Gekomon

MegaKabuterimon (St-28)

Ultimate Level — St-28

Kabuterimon + Digivice
Tortomon + Digivice
Birdramon + Digivice

1st Edition

- 230 DEFEND
- 340 ELECTRO SHOCKER
- 470 HORN BUSTER

Insectoid Digimon
Vaccine

SCORE R:100 C:100 U:100 M:200

© Akiyoshi Hongo • Toei Animation   © 1999 BANDAI

MegaKabuterimon

Triceramon (St-29)

Ultimate Level — St-29

Starmon + Digivice
Monochromon + Digivice
Greymon + Digivice

1st Edition

- 470 TRI-HORN ATTACK
- 430 MEGA DASH
- 250 DEFEND

Dinosaur Digimon
Data

SCORE R:100 C:100 U:100 M:200

© Akiyoshi Hongo • Toei Animation   © 1999 BANDAI

Triceramon

Piximon (St-30)

Ultimate Level — St-30

(DNA) — Tortomon + Gekomon
(DNA) — Monochromon + Starmon
(DNA) — Dokugumon + Rockmon

1st Edition

- 470 PIT BOMB
- 420 MAGICAL TAIL
- 220 DEFEND

Pixie Digimon
Data
Special Ability: Fly

SCORE R:100 C:100 U:100 M:200

© Akiyoshi Hongo • Toei Animation   © 1999 BANDAI

Piximon

Okuwamon

Ultimate Level St-31

Kuwagamon + Digivice
Gekomon + Digivice

1st Edition

290 DEFEND
380 BEETLE HORN ATTACK
400 DOUBLE SCISSOR CLAWS

Insectoid Digimon
Virus
Special Ability: Fly

SCORE **R:100 C:100 U:100 M:200**

© Akiyoshi Hongo • Toei Animation © 1999 BANDAI

☐ Okuwamon

SkullGreymon

Ultimate Level St-32

Kabuterimon + Digivice
Angemon + Digivice
Birdramon + Digivice
Greymon + Digivice

1st Edition

320 DEFEND
430 DARK SHOT
330 DOUBLE DARK SHOT

Skeleton Digimon
Virus

SCORE **R:100 C:100 U:100 M:200**

© Akiyoshi Hongo • Toei Animation © 1999 BANDAI

☐ SkullGreymon

HerculesKabuterimon

Mega Level St-33

MegaKabuterimon + Digivice
Okuwamon + Digivice

1st Edition

300 DEFEND
470 MEGA ELECTRO SHOCKER
510 GIGA SCISSOR CLAW

Insectoid Digimon
Vaccine
Special Ability: Fly
Special Effect: Score 300 when Digivolving to this Digimon.

SCORE **R:100 C:100 U:100 M:100**

© Akiyoshi Hongo • Toei Animation © 1999 BANDAI

☐ HerculesKabuterimon

SaberLeomon

Mega Level St-34

(DNA) — Triceramon + Piximon

1st Edition

550 HOWLING CRUSHER
500 TWIN FANG
310 DEFEND

Ancient Animal Digimon
Data
Special Effect: Score 300 when Digivolving to this Digimon.

SCORE **R:100 C:100 U:100 M:100**

© Akiyoshi Hongo • Toei Animation © 1999 BANDAI

☐ SaberLeomon

Champion Level St-35

Gomamon — offline 1 card
Crabmon — offline 1 card

Dolphmon

1st Edition

● 180 DEFEND
■ 380 DOLPHIN KICK
◆ 400 PULSE BLAST

Sea Animal Digimon
Vaccine
Special Ability: Swim

SCORE R:100 C:100 U:200 M:300

© Akiyoshi Hongo • Toei Animation   © 1999 BANDAI

☐ Dolphmon

Champion Level St-36

Gomamon — offline 2 cards
Crabmon — offline 1 card

Coelamon

1st Edition

● 410 FOSSIL BITE
■ 350 ANCIENT BITE
◆ 190 DEFEND

Ancient Fish Digimon
Data
Special Ability: Swim

SCORE R:100 C:100 U:200 M:300

© Akiyoshi Hongo • Toei Animation   © 1999 BANDAI

☐ Coelamon

Champion Level St-37

Gomamon — offline 2 cards
Syakomon — offline 2 cards

Octomon

1st Edition

● 270 DEFEND
■ 390 SPURTING INK
◆ 360 OCTOPUS TRAP

Mollusk Digimon
Virus
Special Ability: Swim

SCORE R:100 C:100 U:100 M:300

© Akiyoshi Hongo • Toei Animation   © 1999 BANDAI

☐ Octomon

Ultimate Level St-38

Ikkakumon + Digivice
Dolphmon + Digivice
Rockmon + Digivice

Zudomon

1st Edition

● 270 DEFEND
■ 390 HORN & TUSK
◆ 450 VULCAN'S HAMMER

Sea Animal Digimon
Vaccine
Special Ability: Swim

SCORE R:100 C:100 U:100 M:200

© Akiyoshi Hongo • Toei Animation   © 1999 BANDAI

☐ Zudomon

MarineDevimon

Ultimate Level — St-39

Gesomon + Digivice
Octomon + Digivice

1st Edition

- 290 DEFEND
- 450 EVIL WIND
- 400 DARKNESS WATER

Sea Animal Digimon
Virus
Special Ability: Swim

SCORE R:100 C:100 U:100 M:200

© Akiyoshi Hongo • Toei Animation   © 1999 BANDAI

☐ MarineDevimon

Pukumon

Mega Level — St-40

(DNA) — MarineDevimon + Ultimate
(DNA) — Dragomon + Ultimate

1st Edition

- 340 DEFEND
- 480 NEEDLE SQUALL
- 430 GLOBEFISH POISON

Mutant Digimon
Virus
Special Ability: Swim
Special Effect: Score 300 when Digivolving to this Digimon.

SCORE R:100 C:100 U:100 M:100

© Akiyoshi Hongo • Toei Animation   © 1999 BANDAI

☐ Pukumon

Candlemon

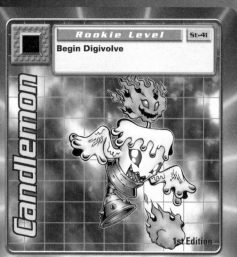

Rookie Level — St-41

Begin Digivolve

1st Edition

- 320 FLAME BOMBER
- 250 MELTED WAX
- 120 DEFEND

Fire Digimon
Data

SCORE R:100 C:200 U:300 M:400

© Akiyoshi Hongo • Toei Animation   © 1999 BANDAI

☐ Candlemon

DemiDevimon

Rookie Level — St-42

Begin Digivolve

1st Edition

- 130 DEFEND
- 250 EVIL WHISPER
- 300 DEMI DART

Evil Digimon
Virus
Special Ability: Fly

SCORE R:100 C:200 U:300 M:400

© Akiyoshi Hongo • Toei Animation   © 1999 BANDAI

☐ DemiDevimon

Apemon

Champion Level St-43

Tapirmon — offline 2 cards
Candlemon — offline 2 cards

1st Edition

- 180 DEFEND
- 370 METALLIC FUR
- 390 MEGA BONE STICK

Animal Digimon
Vaccine

SCORE R:100 C:100 U:200 M:300

© Akiyoshi Hongo • Toei Animation   © 1999 BANDAI

☐ Apemon

Wizardmon

Champion Level St-44

Tapirmon — offline 2 cards
Candlemon — offline 1 card
DemiDevimon — offline 1 card

1st Edition

- 480 THUNDER BLASTER
- 360 MAGICAL GAME
- 200 DEFEND

Wizard Digimon
Data

SCORE R:100 C:100 U:200 M:300

© Akiyoshi Hongo • Toei Animation   © 1999 BANDAI

☐ Wizardmon

Bakemon

Champion Level St-45

DemiDevimon — offline 1 card

1st Edition

- 240 DEFEND
- 390 ZOMBIE CLAW
- 370 EVIL CHARM

Ghost Digimon
Virus
Special Effect: Send
opponent's Digimon
offline when Duel
ends in a tie.

SCORE R:100 C:100 U:100 M:300

© Akiyoshi Hongo • Toei Animation   © 1999 BANDAI

☐ Bakemon

Mammothmon

Ultimate Level St-46

Apemon + Digivice
Garurumon + Digivice

1st Edition

- 230 DEFEND
- 400 FREEZING BREATH
- 440 TUSK CRUSHER

Ancient Animal Digimon
Vaccine

SCORE R:100 C:100 U:100 M:200

© Akiyoshi Hongo • Toei Animation   © 1999 BANDAI

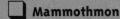

☐ Mammothmon

WereGarurumon

Ultimate Level   St-47

(DNA) — Meramon + Apemon
(DNA) — Garurumon + Wizardmon

1st Edition

- 230 DEFEND
- 400 GARURU KICK
- 470 WOLF CLAW

Animal Digimon
Vaccine

SCORE R:100 C:100 U:100 M:100

© Akiyoshi Hongo • Toei Animation   © 1999 BANDAI

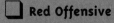 WereGarurumon

SkullMeramon

Ultimate Level   St-48

Meramon + Digivice
Wizardmon + Digivice
Angemon + Digivice

1st Edition

- 480 METAL FIREBALL
- 420 FLAME CHAIN
- 230 DEFEND

Fire Digimon
Data

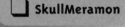

SCORE R:100 C:100 U:100 M:200

© Akiyoshi Hongo • Toei Animation   © 1999 BANDAI

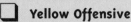 SkullMeramon

Red Offensive

POWER OPTION   St-49
FORCE FX

1st Edition

EFFECT:
Change your Digimon Power to ● (RED).
This does not change your Battle Type.

•Send this card Offline at end of Duel.

© Akiyoshi Hongo • Toei Animation   © 1999 BANDAI

Red Offensive

Yellow Offensive

POWER OPTION   St-50
FORCE FX

1st Edition

EFFECT:
Change your Digimon Power to ◆ (YELLOW).
This does not change your Battle Type.

•Send this card Offline at end of Duel.

© Akiyoshi Hongo • Toei Animation   © 1999 BANDAI

Yellow Offensive

POWER OPTION St-51

FORCE FX

Green Offensive

1st Edition

EFFECT:
Change your Digimon Power to ■ (GREEN).
This does not change your Battle Type.

•Send this card Offline at end of Duel.

© Akiyoshi Hongo • Toei Animation   © 1999 BANDAI

☐ Green Offensive

POWER OPTION St-52

POWER BLAST

Blitz

1st Edition

EFFECT: If you lose the Duel, send
opponent's top three Online cards Offline.

•Send this card Offline at end of Duel.

© Akiyoshi Hongo • Toei Animation   © 1999 BANDA

☐ Blitz

POWER OPTION St-53

POWER BLAST

Metal Attack

1st Edition

EFFECT: Add 50 points to your Digimon
Power. To use this card, send one card from
your hand Offline.

•Send this card Offline at end of Duel.

© Akiyoshi Hongo • Toei Animation   © 1999 BANDAI

☐ Metal Attack

POWER OPTION St-54

POWER BLAST

Counter Attack!

1st Edition

EFFECT: When confronting an opponent of
a higher Digivolve Level, double the number of
your Digimon Power until end of Duel.

•Do not use this card with a Rookie on Duel Zone.
•Send this card Offline at end of Duel.

© Akiyoshi Hongo • Toei Animation   © 1999 BANDA

☐ Counter Attack

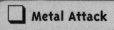
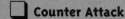

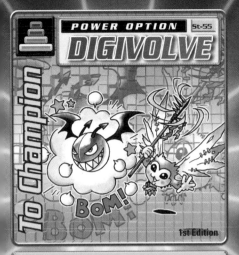

POWER OPTION St-55
DIGIVOLVE
To Champion
1st Edition

EFFECT: Downgrade your Ultimate or Mega to Champion. Place this card face down on Power Port and place Champion from your hand face down on Digivolve Zone.

• Use this card only during Digivolve Phase.

© Akiyoshi Hongo • Toei Animation   © 1999 BANDAI

☐ To Champion

POWER OPTION St-56
DIGIVOLVE
Ultra Digivolve
1st Edition

EFFECT: Digivolve any Digimon to next Level, regardless of Digivolve Requirements. Place this card face down on Power Port and place next–level Digimon face down on Digivolve Zone. To use this card, send the rest of your hand Offline.

• Use this card only during Digivolve Phase.

© Akiyoshi Hongo • Toei Animation   © 1999 BANDAI

☐ Ultra Digivolve

POWER OPTION St-57
POWER BLAST
Downgrade
1st Edition

EFFECT: Downgrade either your Champion or your opponent's Champion to Rookie. Place this card on Power Port and send either your Champion or your opponent's Champion Offline. To use this card, send one card from your hand Offline.

• This effect applies to any player's Digimon.

© Akiyoshi Hongo • Toei Animation   © 1999 BANDAI

☐ Downgrade

POWER OPTION St-58
POWER BLAST
Digi-Duel

Shweet!

1st Edition

EFFECT: If you win the Duel, double your Score. To use this card, send three of your Online cards Offline.

• This card can not be used after opponent passes.
• You may only use one of these cards per Duel.
• Do not use this card with a Rookie in your Duel Zone.
• Send this card Offline at end of Duel.

© Akiyoshi Hongo • Toei Animation   © 1999 BANDAI

☐ Digi-Duel

POWER OPTION | St-61
DIGIVOLVE
Red & Green
Digivice
1st Edition

EFFECT: Use this card when required to Digivolve to an Ultimate or Mega with Battle Type ● [RED] or ■ [GREEN]. Place this card face down on Power Port when placing next-level Digimon face down on Digivolve Zone.

•Use this card only during Digivolve Phase.

© Akiyoshi Hongo • Toei Animation   © 1999 BANDAI

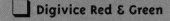

☐ Digivice Red & Green

POWER OPTION | St-62
DIGIVOLVE
Yellow
Digivice
1st Edition

EFFECT: Use this card when required to Digivolve to an Ultimate or Mega with Battle Type ◆ [YELLOW]. Place this card face down on Power Port when placing next-level Digimon face down on Digivolve Zone.

•Use this card only during Digivolve Phase.

© Akiyoshi Hongo • Toei Animation   © 1999 BANDAI

☐ Digivice Yellow

POWER OPTION | St-59
DIGIVOLVE
Red
Digivice
1st Edition

EFFECT: Use this card when required to Digivolve to an Ultimate or Mega with Battle Type ● [RED]. Place this card face down on Power Port when placing next-level Digimon face down on Digivolve Zone.

•Use this card only during Digivolve Phase.

© Akiyoshi Hongo • Toei Animation   © 1999 BANDAI

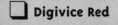

☐ Digivice Red

POWER OPTION | St-60
DIGIVOLVE
Green & Yellow
Digivice
1st Edition

EFFECT: Use this card when required to Digivolve to an Ultimate or Mega with Battle Type ■ [GREEN] or ◆ [YELLOW]. Place this card face down on Power Port when placing next-level Digimon face down on Digivolve Zone.

•Use this card only during Digivolve Phase.

© Akiyoshi Hongo • Toei Animation   © 1999 BANDAI

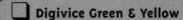

☐ Digivice Green & Yellow

Booster Pack Series 1

Ultimate Level | Bo-01

Greymon + Digivice
Devimon + Digivice

MetalGreymon

● 310
DEFEND
■ 440
GIGA BLASTER
◆ 350
MEGA CLAW

Android Digimon
Virus
Special Ability: Fly

SCORE R:100 C:100 U:100 M:200

© Akiyoshi Hongo • Toei Animation   © 1999 BANDAI

▢ MetalGreymon

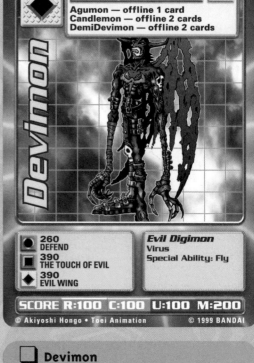

Champion Level | Bo-02

Agumon — offline 1 card
Candlemon — offline 2 cards
DemiDevimon — offline 2 cards

Devimon

● 260
DEFEND
■ 390
THE TOUCH OF EVIL
◆ 390
EVIL WING

Evil Digimon
Virus
Special Ability: Fly

SCORE R:100 C:100 U:100 M:200

© Akiyoshi Hongo • Toei Animation   © 1999 BANDAI

▢ Devimon

30 Leomon — DP 380

Champion Digimon

Leomon

Champion Level — Bo-04
Patamon — offline 2 cards
Kunemon — offline 2 cards

● 250 DEFEND
■ 390 PUMMEL WHACK
◆ 330 BONE CUDGEL

Evil Digimon
Virus

SCORE R:100 C:100 U:100 M:300
© Akiyoshi Hongo • Toei Animation   © 1999 BANDAI

Ogremon

Champion Level — Bo-05
Agumon — offline 2 cards
Tapirmon — offline 1 card
Candlemon — offline 1 card

● 420 FIREBALL
■ 350 ROARING FLAME
◆ 180 DEFEND

Fire Digimon
Data

SCORE R:100 C:100 U:200 M:300
© Akiyoshi Hongo • Toei Animation   © 1999 BANDAI

Meramon

Champion Level — Bo-06
Crabmon — offline 1 card
Syakomon— offline 2 cards

● 420 ICE BLAST
■ 330 ICE WINDER
◆ 220 DEFEND

Sea Animal Digimon
Data
Special Ability: Swim

SCORE R:100 C:100 U:1 00 M:200
© Akiyoshi Hongo • Toei Animation   © 1999 BANDAI

Seadramon

Champion Level Bo-07

Gabumon — offline 2 cards

Frigimon

- ● 220 DEFEND
- ■ 360 SNOW BALL
- ◆ 400 SUBZERO ICE PUNCH

Icy Digimon
Vaccine

SCORE R:100 C:100 U:200 M:300

© Akiyoshi Hongo • Toei Animation   © 1999 BANDAI

☐ Frigimon

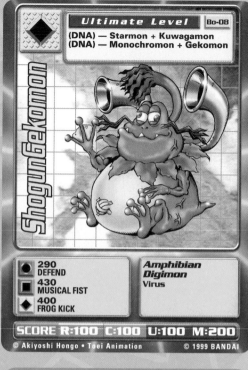

Ultimate Level Bo-08

(DNA) — Starmon + Kuwagamon
(DNA) — Monochromon + Gekomon

ShogunGekomon

- ● 290 DEFEND
- ■ 430 MUSICAL FIST
- ◆ 400 FROG KICK

Amphibian Digimon
Virus

SCORE R:100 C:100 U:100 M:200

© Akiyoshi Hongo • Toei Animation   © 1999 BANDAI

☐ ShogunGekomon

Champion Level Bo-09

Kunemon — offline 1 card

Shellmon

- ● 400 HYDRO BLASTER
- ■ 350 SLAMMING ATTACK
- ◆ 180 DEFEND

Sea Animal Digimon
Data
Special Ability:
Swim, Dig

SCORE R:100 C:100 U:100 M:300

© Akiyoshi Hongo • Toei Animation   © 1999 BANDAI

☐ Shellmon

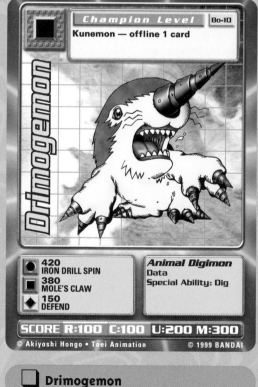

Champion Level Bo-10

Kunemon — offline 1 card

Drimogemon

- ● 420 IRON DRILL SPIN
- ■ 380 MOLE'S CLAW
- ◆ 150 DEFEND

Animal Digimon
Data
Special Ability: Dig

SCORE R:100 C:100 U:200 M:300

© Akiyoshi Hongo • Toei Animation   © 1999 BANDAI

☐ Drimogemon

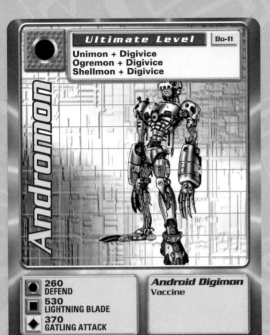

Ultimate Level   Bo-11

Unimon + Digivice
Ogremon + Digivice
Shellmon + Digivice

Andromon

● 260 DEFEND
■ 530 LIGHTNING BLADE
◆ 370 GATLING ATTACK

Android Digimon
Vaccine

SCORE R:100 C:100 U:100 M:200

© Akiyoshi Hongo • Toei Animation   © 1999 BANDAI

☐ Andromon

Champion Level   Bo-12

Biyomon — offline 2 cards
Gotsumon — offline 2 cards

Monochromon

● 440 VOLCANIC STRIKE
■ 360 SLAMMING ATTACK
◆ 190 DEFEND

Dinosaur Digimon
Data

SCORE R:100 C:100 U:200 M:300

© Akiyoshi Hongo • Toei Animation   © 1999 BANDAI

☐ Monochromon

Champion Level   Bo-13

Biyomon — offline 2 cards
Palmon — offline 2 cards
Tentomon — offline 2 cards

Kuwagamon

● 240 DEFEND
■ 380 SCISSOR CLAW
◆ 340 POWER GUILLOTINE

Insectoid Digimon
Virus
Special Ability: Fly

SCORE R:100 C:100 U:100 M:300

© Akiyoshi Hongo • Toei Animation   © 1999 BANDAI

☐ Kuwagamon

Champion Level   Bo-14

Palmon — offline 2 cards

Mojyamon

● 180 DEFEND
■ 370 BONE BOOMERANG
◆ 390 ICE CLOUD

Rare Animal Digimon
Vaccine

SCORE R:100 C:100 U:200 M:300

© Akiyoshi Hongo • Toei Animation   © 1999 BANDAI

☐ Mojyamon

Champion Level Bo-15

Tentomon — offline 1 card
Gotsumon — offline 1 card
Otamamon — offline 2 cards

Gatomon

210 DEFEND
360 CAT'S EYE HYPNOTISM
370 LIGHTNING CLAW

Animal Digimon
Vaccine

SCORE **R:100 C:100 U:100 M:100**

© Akiyoshi Hongo • Toei Animation   © 1999 BANDAI

☐ **Gatomon**

Ultimate Level Bo-16

(DNA) — Kabuterimon + Monochromon
(DNA) — Gatomon + Starmon

Angewomon

260 DEFEND
400 HEAVEN'S CHARM
470 CELESTIAL ARROW

Angel Digimon
Vaccine
Special Ability: Fly

SCORE **R:100 C:100 U:100 M:100**

© Akiyoshi Hongo • Toei Animation   © 1999 BANDAI

☐ **Angewomon**

Mega Level Bo-17

MegaKabuterimon + Digivice
Okuwamon + Digivice
Angewomon + Digivice

Magnadramon

350 DEFEND
520 DRAGON FIRE
540 FIRE TORNADO

Holy Dragon Digimon
Vaccine
Special Ability: Fly
Special Effect: Score 300 when Digivolving to this Digimon.

SCORE **R:100 C:100 U:100 M:100**

© Akiyoshi Hongo • Toei Animation   © 1999 BANDAI

☐ **Magnadramon**

Champion Level Bo-18

Gomamon — offline 2 cards
Crabmon — offline 1 card

Ebidramon

420 TWIN SCISSORS
340 LOBSTER STEP
190 DEFEND

Sea Animal Digimon
Data
Special Ability: Swim

SCORE **R:100 C:100 U:200 M:300**

© Akiyoshi Hongo • Toei Animation   © 1999 BANDAI

☐ **Ebidramon**

Champion Level   Bo-19
Agumon — offline 2 cards
Gabumon — offline 2 cards

Gorillamon

430 POWER LIFTING
340 ENERGY BLASTER
180 DEFEND

Animal Digimon
Data

SCORE R:100 C:100 U:100 M:300

© Akiyoshi Hongo • Toei Animation   © 1999 BANDAI

Gorillamon

Champion Level   Bo-20
Biyomon — offline 2 cards
DemiDevimon — offline 2 cards

Vilemon

230 DEFEND
330 SCRATCH
370 NIGHTMARE SHOCKER

Evil Digimon
Virus
Special Ability: Fly

SCORE R:100 C:100 U:100 M:300

© Akiyoshi Hongo • Toei Animation   © 1999 BANDAI

Vilemon

Ultimate Level   Bo-21
Ogremon + Digivice
Leomon + Digivice

Minotarumon

280 DEFEND
400 BULL FIGHTING ATTACK
410 DARKSIDE QUAKE

Animal Digimon
Virus

SCORE R:100 C:100 U:100 M:300

© Akiyoshi Hongo • Toei Animation   © 1999 BANDAI

Minotarumon

Ultimate Level   Bo-22
Devimon + Digivice
Angemon + Digivice

LadyDevimon

300 DEFEND
410 EVIL WING
420 DARKNESS WAVE

Evil Digimon
Virus
Special Ability: Fly

SCORE R:100 C:100 U:100 M:100

© Akiyoshi Hongo • Toei Animation   © 1999 BANDAI

LadyDevimon

Roachmon — Bo-23

Champion Level Bo-23

Kunemon — offline 2 cards
Tentomon — offline 2 cards

- 220 DEFEND
- 300 FLYING ATTACK
- 390 DREAM DUST

Insectoid Digimon
Virus
Special Ability: Fly

SCORE R:100 C:100 U:200 M:300

© Akiyoshi Hongo • Toei Animation   © 1999 BANDAI

☐ Roachmon

Asuramon — Bo-24

Ultimate Level Bo-24

Unimon + Digivice
Ogremon + Digivice
Shellmon + Digivice

- 260 DEFEND
- 520 THE FIST OF ASURA
- 430 MULTIPLE FACES

Wizard Digimon
Vaccine

SCORE R:100 C:100 U:100 M:100

© Akiyoshi Hongo • Toei Animation   © 1999 BANDAI

☐ Asuramon

Snimon — Bo-25

Champion Level Bo-25

Gabumon — offline 2 cards

- 200 DEFEND
- 350 SLAMMING ATTACK
- 410 TWIN SICKLES

Insectoid Digimon
Vaccine

SCORE R:100 C:100 U:200 M:300

© Akiyoshi Hongo • Toei Animation   © 1999 BANDAI

☐ Snimon

Jagamon — Bo-26

Ultimate Level Bo-26

(DNA) — Kabuterimon + Monochromon
(DNA) — Tortomon + Starmon

- 240 DEFEND
- 420 FRIED POTATO
- 430 POTATO SMASH

Vegetation Digimon
Vaccine

SCORE R:100 C:100 U:100 M:200

© Akiyoshi Hongo • Toei Animation   © 1999 BANDAI

☐ Jagamon

Crabmon

Rookie Level	**Bo-28**

Begin Digivolve

- 340 SCISSOR MAGIC
- 250 CRAB MEAT BOMBER
- 110 DEFEND

Crustacean Digimon
Data
Special Ability: Dig

SCORE R:100 C:200 U:300 M:400

Crabmon

Syakomon

Rookie Level	**Bo-29**

Begin Digivolve

- 140 DEFEND
- 250 WATER PRESSURE
- 300 BLACK PEARL BLAST

Crustacean Digimon
Virus
Special Ability: Swim

SCORE R:100 C:200 U:300 M:400

Syakomon

Gesomon

Champion Level	**Bo-30**

Syakomon — offline 2 cards
Crabmon — offline 2 cards

- 240 DEFEND
- 380 CORAL CRUSHER
- 330 ELASTIC ARMS

Mollusk Digimon
Virus
Special Ability: Swim

SCORE R:100 C:100 U:100 M:300

Gesomon

MegaSeadramon

Ultimate Level	**Bo-31**

Seadramon + Digivice
Coelamon + Digivice

- 470 THUNDER JAVELIN
- 420 MEGA ICE BLAST
- 210 DEFEND

Sea Animal Digimon
Data
Special Ability: Swim

SCORE R:100 C:100 U:100 M:200

MegaSeadramon

Scorpiomon (Bo-32)

Ultimate Level

(DNA) — Coelamon + Seadramon
(DNA) — Gesomon + Ikkakumon
(DNA) — Octomon + Dolphmon

- ● 470 TAIL BLADE
- ■ 430 TWIN SWORD
- ◆ 220 DEFEND

Crustacean Digimon
Data
Special Ability: Swim

SCORE R:100 C:100 U:100 M:200

© Akiyoshi Hongo • Toei Animation   © 1999 BANDAI

☐ Scorpiomon

Dragomon (Bo-33)

Ultimate Level

(DNA) — Gesomon + Seadramon
(DNA) — Octomon + Coelamon

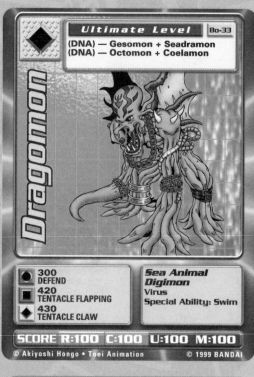

- ● 300 DEFEND
- ■ 420 TENTACLE FLAPPING
- ◆ 430 TENTACLE CLAW

Sea Animal Digimon
Virus
Special Ability: Swim

SCORE R:100 C:100 U:100 M:100

© Akiyoshi Hongo • Toei Animation   © 1999 BANDAI

☐ Dragomon

MarineAngemon (Bo-34)

Mega Level

MegaSeadramon + Digivice
Zudomon + Digivice

- ● 310 DEFEND
- ■ 470 SMILING FACE
- ◆ 570 OCEAN LOVE

Pixie Digimon
Vaccine
Special Ability: Swim
Special Effect: Score 300 when Digivolving to this Digimon.

SCORE R:100 C:100 U:100 M:100

© Akiyoshi Hongo • Toei Animation   © 1999 BANDAI

☐ MarineAngemon

MetalSeadramon (Bo-35)

Mega Level

(DNA) — Scorpiomon + MegaSeadramon

- ● 550 RIVER OF POWER
- ■ 480 GIGA ICE BLAST
- ◆ 330 DEFEND

Android Digimon
Data
Special Ability: Swim
Special Effect: Score 300 when Digivolving to this Digimon.

SCORE R:100 C:100 U:100 M:100

© Akiyoshi Hongo • Toei Animation   © 1999 BANDAI

☐ MetalSeadramon

Rookie Level — Bo-36

Begin Digivolve

Tapirmon

- ● 140 DEFEND
- ■ 220 DELETING VIRUS
- ◆ 350 WAKING DREAM

Animal Digimon
Vaccine

SCORE R:100 C:200 U:300 M:400

© Akiyoshi Hongo • Toei Animation   © 1999 BANDAI

☐ Tapirmon

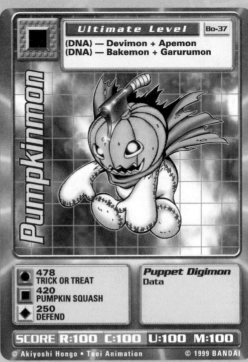

Ultimate Level — Bo-37

(DNA) — Devimon + Apemon
(DNA) — Bakemon + Garurumon

Pumpkinmon

- ● 478 TRICK OR TREAT
- ■ 420 PUMPKIN SQUASH
- ◆ 250 DEFEND

Puppet Digimon
Data

SCORE R:100 C:100 U:100 M:100

© Akiyoshi Hongo • Toei Animation   © 1999 BANDAI

☐ Pumpkinmon

Ultimate Level — Bo-38

Devimon + Digivice
Bakemon + Digivice

Myotismon

- ● 280 DEFEND
- ■ 350 NIGHTMARE CLAW
- ◆ 410 GRISLY WING

Ghost Digimon
Virus

SCORE R:100 C:100 U:100 M:100

© Akiyoshi Hongo • Toei Animation   © 1999 BANDAI

☐ Myotismon

Ultimate Level — Bo-39

(DNA) — Devimon + Meremon
(DNA) — Bakemon + Wizardmon

Phantomon

- ● 300 DEFEND
- ■ 400 FATHER TIME
- ◆ 430 SHADOW SCYTHE

Ghost Digimon
Virus

SCORE R:100 C:100 U:100 M:100

© Akiyoshi Hongo • Toei Animation   © 1999 BANDAI

☐ Phantomon

SkullMammothmon

Mega Level   Bo-40

Mammothmon + Digivice
Myotismon + Digivice

- 360 DEFEND
- 480 DASH
- 520 SPIRAL BONE CRUSHER

Ghost Digimon
Vaccine
Special Effect: Score 300 when Digivolving to this Digimon.

SCORE **R:100** **C:100** **U:100** **M:100**

© Akiyoshi Hongo • Toei Animation   © 1999 BANDAI

☐ SkullMammothmon

Boltmon

Mega Level   Bo-41

(DNA) — SkullMeramon + Pumpkinmon

- 570 TOMAHAWK CRUNCH
- 490 TOMAHAWK KNUCKLE
- 280 DEFEND

Android Digimon
Data
Special Effect: Score 300 when Digivolving to this Digimon.

SCORE **R:100** **C:100** **U:100** **M:100**

© Akiyoshi Hongo • Toei Animation   © 1999 BANDAI

☐ Boltmon

Piedmon

Mega Level   Bo-42

(DNA) — Myotismon + ULTIMATE
(DNA) — Phantomon + ULTIMATE

- 340 DEFEND
- 490 CROWN TRICK
- 530 TRUMP SWORD

Wizard Digimon
Virus
Special Effect: Score 300 when Digivolving to this Digimon.

SCORE **R:100** **C:100** **U:100** **M:100**

© Akiyoshi Hongo • Toei Animation   © 1999 BANDAI

☐ Piedmon

Fly-Trap

POWER OPTION   Bo-43

POWER BLAST

EFFECT: When confronting an opponent with Special Ability "Fly", add 50 points to your Digimon Power.

• Effect applies until voided by opponent or sent Offline by you.

© Akiyoshi Hongo • Toei Animation   © 1999 BANDAI

☐ Fly-Trap

POWER OPTION — Bo-44
POWER BLAST
Coral Rip

EFFECT: When confronting an opponent with Special Ability "Swim", add 50 points to your Digimon Power.

• Effect applies until voided by opponent or sent Offline by you.

© Akiyoshi Hongo • Toei Animation   © 1999 BANDAI

☐ Coral Rip

POWER OPTION — Bo-45
POWER BLAST
Aquatic Attack

EFFECT: Your Digimon acquires Special Ability "Swim", and adds 20 points to your Digimon Power.

• Effect applies until voided by opponent or sent Offline by you.

© Akiyoshi Hongo • Toei Animation   © 1999 BANDAI

☐ Aquatic Attack

POWER OPTION — Bo-46
POWER BLAST
Fly Away

EFFECT: Your Digimon acquires Special Ability "Fly", and adds 20 points to your Digimon Power.

• Effect applies until voided by opponent or sent Offline by you.

© Akiyoshi Hongo • Toei Animation   © 1999 BANDAI

☐ Fly Away

POWER OPTION — Bo-47
POWER BLAST
Iron Drill

EFFECT: Your Digimon acquires Special Ability "Dig", and adds 20 points to your Digimon Power.

• Effect applies until voided by opponent or sent Offline by you.

© Akiyoshi Hongo • Toei Animation   © 1999 BANDAI

☐ Iron Drill

POWER OPTION Bo-48
POWER BLAST
Organic Enhancer

EFFECT: Add 20 points to your Digimon Power when your Digimon Group is Vegetation or Insectoid.

• Effect applies until voided by opponent or sent Offline by you.

© Akiyoshi Hongo • Toei Animation   © 1999 BANDAI

☐ Organic Enhancer

POWER OPTION Bo-49
POWER BLAST
Option Eater

EFFECT: Void opponent's Power Blast or Force FX card and send it Offline.

• Send this card Offline after use.

© Akiyoshi Hongo • Toei Animation   © 1999 BANDAI

☐ Option Eater

POWER OPTION Bo-50
POWER BLAST
Power Freeze

EFFECT: Void opponent's Digivolve or Force FX card and send it Offline.

• Send this card Offline after use.

© Akiyoshi Hongo • Toei Animation   © 1999 BANDAI

☐ Power Freeze

POWER OPTION Bo-51
POWER BLAST
Even Steven

EFFECT: Stop the Duel. All Digimon remain on Duel Zone and all Power Option cards go Offline. No points scored.

• Send this card Offline after use.

© Akiyoshi Hongo • Toei Animation   © 1999 BANDAI

☐ Even Steven

POWER OPTION Bo-52
POWER BLAST
Bomb Dive

EFFECT: When confronting an opponent with Battle Type ■ (Green) or ◆ (Yellow), add 100 points to your Digimon Power until end of Duel. To use this card, you need Special Ability "Fly".

• Send this card Offline at end of Duel.

© Akiyoshi Hongo • Toei Animation   © 1999 BANDAI

☐ **Bomb Dive**

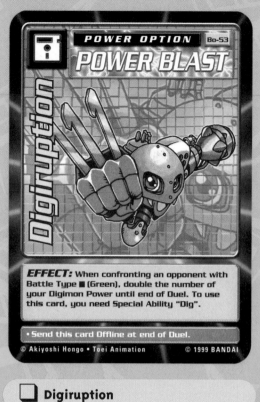

POWER OPTION Bo-53
POWER BLAST
Digiruption

EFFECT: When confronting an opponent with Battle Type ■ (Green), double the number of your Digimon Power until end of Duel. To use this card, you need Special Ability "Dig".

• Send this card Offline at end of Duel.

© Akiyoshi Hongo • Toei Animation   © 1999 BANDAI

☐ **Digiruption**

POWER OPTION Bo-54
POWER BLAST
Depth Charge

EFFECT: When confronting an opponent with Battle Type ● (Red), reduce by half the number of your opponent's Digimon Power until end of Duel. To use this card, you need Special Ability "Swim".

• Send this card Offline at end of Duel.

© Akiyoshi Hongo • Toei Animation   © 1999 BANDAI

☐ **Depth Charge**

Booster Pack Series 2

Mega Level	Bo-55

MetalGreymon + Digivice
Megadramon + Digivice
AeroVeedramon + Digivice

Machinedramon

- 340 DEFEND
- 490 DRAGON FIRE
- 510 GIGA CANNON

Android Digimon
Virus
Special Effect: Score 300 when Digivolving to this Digimon

SCORE **R:100** **C:100** **U:100** **M:100**

© Akiyoshi Hongo • Toei Animation   © 1999 BANDAI

Champion Level	Bo-56

Biyomon — offline 2 cards

Kokatorimon

- 440 FROZEN FIRE SHOT
- 360 FEATHER SWORD
- 190 DEFEND

Bird Digimon
Data

SCORE **R:100** **C:100** **U:100** **M:300**

© Akiyoshi Hongo • Toei Animation   © 1999 BANDAI

 Machinedramon   ☐ Kokatorimon

Ultimate Level | Bo-57

Sukamon + Digivice

Etemon

- ● 300 DEFEND
- ■ 420 MONKEY CLAW
- ◆ 440 DARK NETWORK & CONCERT CRUSH

Puppet Digimon
Virus

SCORE R:100 C:100 U:100 M:100

© Akiyoshi Hongo • Toei Animation   © 1999 BANDAI

☐ Etemon

Champion Level | Bo-58

Gomamon — offline 1 card
Elecmon— offline 2 cards

Whamon

- ● 180 DEFEND
- ■ 360 TIDAL WAVE
- ◆ 410 BLASTING SPOUT

Sea Animal Digimon
Vaccine
Special Ability: Swim

SCORE R:100 C:100 U:200 M:300

© Akiyoshi Hongo • Toei Animation   © 1999 BANDAI

☐ Whamon

Champion Level | Bo-59

Patamon— offline 1 card
Kunemon— offline 1 card

Sukamon

- ● 100 DEFEND
- ■ 160 SMASH
- ◆ 300 BOMBER

Mutant Digimon
Virus
Special Effect: Add 100 to your score when this Digimon wins

SCORE R:100 C:200 U:300 M:400

© Akiyoshi Hongo • Toei Animation   © 1999 BANDAI

☐ Sukamon

Rookie Level | Bo-60

Begin Digivolve

Gazimon

- ● 180 DEFEND
- ■ 250 PITFALL
- ◆ 320 ELECTRIC STUN BLAST

Mammal Digimon
Virus
Special Ability: Dig

SCORE R:100 C:200 U:300 M:400

© Akiyoshi Hongo • Toei Animation   © 1999 BANDAI

☐ Gazimon

Elecmon — Bo-61

Rookie Level
Begin Digivolve

- 340 SPARKLING THUNDER
- 260 BODY ATTACK
- 140 DEFEND

Mammal Digimon
Data
Special Ability: Dig

SCORE R:100 C:200 U:300 M:400

© Akiyoshi Hongo • Toei Animation   © 1999 BANDAI

Elecmon

Monzaemon — Bo-62

Ultimate Level
Numemon + Digivice

- 250 DEFEND
- 400 HUG
- 470 HEARTS ATTACK

Puppet Digimon
Vaccine

SCORE R:100 C:100 U:100 M:200

© Akiyoshi Hongo • Toei Animation   © 1999 BANDAI

Monzaemon

Mamemon — Bo-64

Ultimate Level
Greymon + Digivice
Meramon + Digivice
Seadramon + Digivice

- 450 SMILEY BOMB
- 390 SPARKLING BLOW
- 220 DEFEND

Mutant Digimon
Data
Special Ability: Dig

SCORE R:100 C:100 U:100 M:200

© Akiyoshi Hongo • Toei Animation   © 1999 BANDAI

Mamemon

MetalMamemon — Bo-65

Ultimat Level
Garurumon + Digivice
Frigimon + Digivice
Whamon + Digivice

- 460 ENERGETIC BOMB
- 410 METAL CLAW
- 250 DEFEND

Android Digimon
Data

SCORE R:100 C:100 U:100 M:200

© Akiyoshi Hongo • Toei Animation   © 1999 BANDAI

MetalMamemon

Champion Level   Bo-66

Agumon— offline 2 cards

Tyrannomon

420 FIRE BLAST
360 SCRATCH
190 DEFEND

Dinosaur Digimon
Data

SCORE R:100 C:100 U:200 M:300

© Akiyoshi Hongo • Toei Animation   © 1999 BANDAI

☐ Tyrannomon

Ultimate Level   Bo-67

Cyclonemon + Digivice
Tuskmon + Digivice
Deltamon + Digivice

Datamon

280 DEFEND
380 DIGITAL BOMB
340 DATA CRUSHER

Machine Digimon
Virus

SCORE R:100 C:100 U:100 M:200

© Akiyoshi Hongo • Toei Animation   © 1999 BANDAI

☐ Datamon

Ultimate Level   Bo-68

Centarumon + Digivice
Bakemon + Digivice
Drimogemon + Digivice

Giromon

230 DEFEND
390 CHAIN SAW
460 BIG BANG BOOM

Machine Digimon
Vaccine

SCORE R:100 C:100 U:100 M:200

© Akiyoshi Hongo • Toei Animation   © 1999 BANDAI

☐ Giromon

Ultimate Level   Bo-69

Monochromon + Digivice
Leomon + Digivice
Coelamon + Digivice

Megadramon

300 DEFEND
420 DARK SIDE ATTACK
390 ULTIMATE SLICER

Dark Dragon Digimon
Virus
Special Ability: Fly

SCORE R:100 C:100 U:100 M:200

© Akiyoshi Hongo • Toei Animation   © 1999 BANDAI

☐ Megadramon

Digitamamon

Ultimate Level   Bo-70

Nanimon + Digivice

- 480 NIGHTMARE SYNDROME
- 410 HYPER FLASHING
- 290 DEFEND

Perfect Digimon
Data

SCORE **R:100 C:100 U:100 M:200**

© Akiyoshi Hongo • Toei Animation   © 1999 BANDAI

☐ **Digitamamon**

Gizamon

Rookie Level   Bo-71

Begin Digivolve

- 160 DEFEND
- 250 4-LEG KICK
- 340 SPIRAL SAW

Sea Animal Digimon
Virus
Special Abilities:
Swim, Dig

SCORE **R:100 C:200 U:300 M:400**

© Akiyoshi Hongo • Toei Animation   © 1999 BANDAI

☐ **Gizamon**

Raremon

Champion Level   Bo-72

Gazimon — offline 1 card
Gizamon — offline 1 card

- 140 DEFEND
- 280 STINKING GAS
- 390 BREATH OF DECAY

Ghost Digimon
Virus
Special Effect: Send 1 card from opponent's Online to Offline when this Digimon wins.

SCORE **R:100 C:100 U:200 M:300**

© Akiyoshi Hongo • Toei Animation   © 1999 BANDAI

☐ **Raremon**

ExTyrannomon

Ultimate Level   Bo-73

Raremon + Digivice

- 240 DEFEND
- 410 DANGEROUS ZIPPER
- 500 PRETTY ATTACK

Puppet Digimon
Vaccine

SCORE **R:100 C:100 U:100 M:100**

© Akiyoshi Hongo • Toei Animation   © 1999 BANDAI

☐ **ExTyrannomon**

Deltamon

Champion Level — Bo-74

Gizamon — offline 2 cards

230 DEFEND
390 TRIPLE FORCES
340 SERPENT BITE

Composition Digimon
Virus

SCORE R:100 C:100 U:100 M:300

© Akiyoshi Hongo • Tōei Animation   © 1999 BANDAI

☐ Deltamon

Tuskmon

Champion Level — Bo-75

Gazimon — offline 2 cards
Gizamon — offline 2 cards

240 DEFEND
400 HORN BUSTER
410 SLAMMING TUSK

Dinosaur Digimon
Virus

SCORE R:100 C:100 U:100 M:300

© Akiyoshi Hongo • Tōei Animation   © 1999 BANDAI

☐ Tuskmon

Myotismon

Ultimate Level — Bo-76

Devimon + Digivice
Bakemon + Digivice

310 DEFEND
380 NIGHTMARE CLAW
420 GRISLY WING

Ghost Digimon
Virus

SCORE R:100 C:100 U:100 M:100

© Akiyoshi Hongo • Tōei Animation   © 1999 BANDAI

☐ Myotismon

Gatomon

Champion Level — Bo-77

Patamon — offline 2 cards
Gazimon — offline 2 cards
Elecmon — offline 2 cards

220 DEFEND
370 CAT'S EYE HYPNOTISM
400 LIGHTNING CLAW

Animal Digimon
Vaccine

SCORE R:100 C:100 U:100 M:300

© Akiyoshi Hongo • Tōei Animation   © 1999 BANDAI

☐ Gatomon

Cyclonemon

Champion Level Bo-78

Gazimon — offline 2 cards

- 300 DEFEND
- 400 HYPER HEAT
- 400 ARM BOMBER

Dragon Digimon
Virus

SCORE **R:100 C:100 U:100 M:200**

© Akiyoshi Hongo • Toei Animation   © 1999 BANDAI

☐ Cyclonemon

DarkTyrannomon

Champion Level Bo-79

Gazimon — offline 2 cards

- 270 DEFEND
- 350 IRON TAIL
- 390 FIRE BLAST

Dinosaur Digimon
Virus

SCORE **R:100 C:100 U:100 M:300**

© Akiyoshi Hongo • Toei Animation   © 1999 BANDAI

☐ DarkTyrannomon

MetalGreymon

Ultimate Level Bo-80

Greymon + Digivice
Veedramon + Digivice

- 290 DEFEND
- 440 MEGA CLAW
- 440 GIGA BLASTER

Android Digimon
Vaccine
Special Ability: Fly

SCORE **R:100 C:100 U:100 M:200**

© Akiyoshi Hongo • Toei Animation   © 1999 BANDAI

☐ MetalGreymon

Floramon

Rookie Level Bo-81

Begin Digivolve

- 330 RAIN OF POLLEN
- 260 STAMEN ROPE
- 170 DEFEND

Vegetation Digimon
Data

SCORE **R:100 C:200 U:300 M:400**

© Akiyoshi Hongo • Toei Animation   © 1999 BANDAI

☐ Floramon

Mushroomon

Rookie Level — Bo-82

Begin Digivolve

160 DEFEND
250 LAUGHING SMASHER
310 FUNGUS CRUNCHER

Vegetation Digimon
Virus

SCORE R:100 C:200 U:300 M:400

© Akiyoshi Hongo • Toei Animation   © 1999 BANDAI

☐ Mushroomon

Veedramon

Champion Level — Bo-83

Biyomon — offline 2 cards
Mushroomon — offline 2 cards

200 DEFEND
350 HAMMER PUNCH
430 V-NOVA BLAST

Mythical Animal Digimon
Vaccine

SCORE R:100 C:100 U:200 M:300

© Akiyoshi Hongo • Toei Animation   © 1999 BANDAI

☐ Veedramon

Togemon

Champion Level — Bo-84

Palmon — offline 2 cards
Floramon — offline 2 cards
Biyomon — offline 2 cards

380 NEEDLE SPRAY
300 LIGHTSPEED JABBING
180 DEFEND

Vegetation Digimon
Data

SCORE R:100 C:100 U:200 M:300

© Akiyoshi Hongo • Toei Animation   © 1999 BANDAI

☐ Togemon

Kiwimon

Champion Level — Bo-85

Floramon — offline 1 card

400 PUMMEL PECK
350 HIGH JUMPING KICK
150 DEFEND

Ancient Bird Digimon
Data

SCORE R:100 C:100 U:200 M:300

© Akiyoshi Hongo • Toei Animation   © 1999 BANDAI

☐ Kiwimon

Woodmon

Champion Level   Bo-86

Floramon — offline 2 cards
Biyomon — offline 1 card
Mushroomon — offline 2 cards

- 240 DEFEND
- 380 TWIG TAP
- 360 WOODY SMASHER

Vegetation Digimon
Virus

SCORE R:100 C:100 U:100 M:300

© Akiyoshi Hongo • Toei Animation   © 1999 BANDAI

☐ Woodmon

RedVegiemon

Champion Level   Bo-87

Floramon — offline 2 cards
Mushroomon — offline 1 card

- 260 DEFEND
- 350 POISON IVY
- 370 ROTTEN RAINBALLS

Vegetation Digimon
Virus
Special Ability: Dig

SCORE R:100 C:100 U:100 M:300

© Akiyoshi Hongo • Toei Animation   © 1999 BANDAI

☐ RedVegiemon

AeroVeedramon

Ultimate Level   Bo-88

Veedramon + Digivice
Birdramon + Digivice

- 280 DEFEND
- 450 V-WING BLADE
- 440 MAGNUM CRASHER

Holy Dragon Digimon
Vaccine
Special Ability: Fly

SCORE R:100 C:100 U:100 M:200

© Akiyoshi Hongo • Toei Animation   © 1999 BANDAI

☐ AeroVeedramon

Garudamon

Ultimate Level   Bo-89

(DNA) — Togemon + Veedramon
(DNA) — Birdramon + Kiwimon
(DNA) — Veedramon + Birdramon

- 260 DEFEND
- 460 WING BLADE
- 430 EAGLE CLAW

Bird Digimon
Vaccine
Special Ability: Fly

SCORE R:100 C:100 U:100 M:200

© Akiyoshi Hongo • Toei Animation   © 1999 BANDAI

☐ Garudamon

Blossomon

Ultimate Level | Bo-90

Togemon + Digivice
Kiwimon + Digivice

- 460 SPIRAL FLOWER
- 400 THORN WHIPS
- 230 DEFEND

Vegetation Digimon
Data

SCORE R:100 C:100 U:100 M:200

© Akiyoshi Hongo • Toei Animation   © 1999 BANDAI

☐ Blossomon

Deramon

Ultimate Level | Bo-91

(DNA) — Veedramon + Woodmon
(DNA) — Birdramon + RedVegiemon

- 470 ROYAL SMASHER
- 430 BEAK BUSTER
- 240 DEFEND

Bird Digimon
Data

SCORE R:100 C:100 U:100 M:200

© Akiyoshi Hongo • Toei Animation   © 1999 BANDAI

☐ Deramon

Cherrymon

Ultimate Level | Bo-92

Woodmon + Digivice
RedVegiemon + Digivice

- 300 DEFEND
- 450 PIT PELTER
- 410 ILLUSION MIST

Vegetation Digimon
Virus

SCORE R:100 C:100 U:100 M:100

© Akiyoshi Hongo • Toei Animation   © 1999 BANDAI

☐ Cherrymon

Garbagemon

Ultimate Level | Bo-93

(DNA) — Togemon + Woodmon
(DNA) — Kiwimon + RedVegiemon

- 280 DEFEND
- 370 DIRTY SAUCER
- 430 JUNK CHUNKER

Mutant Digimon
Virus

SCORE R:100 C:100 U:100 M:200

© Akiyoshi Hongo • Toei Animation   © 1999 BANDAI

☐ Garbagemon

Phoenixmon

Mega Level Bo-94

AeroVeedramon + Digivice
Garudamon + Digivice
Deramon + Digivice

- ● 350 DEFEND
- ■ 530 CRIMSON FLAME
- ◆ 530 STAR-LIGHT EXPLOSION

Animal Digimon
Vaccine
Special Ability: Fly
Special Effect: Score 300 when Digivolving to this Digimon

SCORE R:100 C:100 U:100 M:100

© Akiyoshi Hongo • Toei Animation   © 1999 BANDAI

☐ Phoenixmon

Gryphonmon

Mega Level Bo-95

(DNA) — Blossomon + Deramon

- ● 580 LEGENDARY BLADE
- ■ 480 LEGENDARY CLAW
- ◆ 300 DEFEND

Mythical Animal Digimon
Data
Special Ability: Fly,Dig
Special Effect: Score 300 when Digivolving to this Digimon

SCORE R:100 C:100 U:100 M:100

© Akiyoshi Hongo • Toei Animation   © 1999 BANDAI

☐ Gryphonmon

Puppetmon

Mega Level Bo-96

(DNA) — Cherrymon + ULTIMATE
(DNA) — Garbagemon + ULTIMATE

- ● 340 DEFEND
- ■ 460 LIE
- ◆ 490 PUPPET PUMMEL

Puppet Digimon
Virus
Special Effect: Score 300 when Digivolving to this Digimon

SCORE R:100 C:100 U:100 M:100

© Akiyoshi Hongo • Toei Animation   © 1999 BANDAI

☐ Puppetmon

POWER OPTION Bo-97
DIGIVOLVE
Green

EFFECT: Use this card when required to Digivolve to an Ultimate or Mega with Battle Type ■ (GREEN). Place this card face down on Power Port when placing next-level Digimon face down on Digivolve Zone.

• Use this card only during Digivolve Phase.

© Akiyoshi Hongo • Toei Animation   © 1999 BANDAI

☐ Digivice Green

POWER OPTION Bo-98
DIGIVOLVE
Red & Yellow
Digivice

EFFECT: Use this card when required to Digivolve to an Ultimate or Mega with Battle Type ● (RED) or ◆ (YELLOW). Place this card face down on Power Port when placing next-level Digimon face down on Digivolve Zone.

• Use this card only during Digivolve Phase.

© Akiyoshi Hongo • Toei Animation   © 1999 BANDAI

☐ Digivice Red & Yellow

POWER OPTION Bo-99
DIGIVOLVE
Crest Tag

EFFECT: Digivolve Champion to Ultimate, regardless of it Digivolve Requirements. Place this card face down on Power Port and place Ultimate Digimon face down on Digivolve Zone.

• Effect applies until end of Duel.
• Card remains on Power Port until you either choose to send it Offline, lose a Duel, get voided by opponent, or your Online deck is reduced to zero.

© Akiyoshi Hongo • Toei Animation   © 1999 BANDAI

☐ Crest Tag

POWER OPTION Bo-100
POWER BLAST
Crest of Courage

EFFECT: Add 50 points to your Digimon Power. If you place this card on "Crest Tag", acquire Special Ability "Fly" and add an additional 50 points to your ■ (GREEN) Digimon Power (regardless of opponent's Battle Type).

• Send this card Offline at end of Duel.

© Akiyoshi Hongo • Toei Animation   © 1999 BANDAI

☐ Crest of Courage

POWER OPTION Bo-101
POWER BLAST
Crest of Reliability

EFFECT: Add 50 points to your Digimon Power. If you place this card on "Crest Tag" and you are "Sea Animal Digimon", add an additional 50 points to your Digimon Power.

• Send this card Offline at end of Duel.

© Akiyoshi Hongo • Toei Animation   © 1999 BANDAI

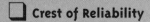
☐ Crest of Reliability

POWER OPTION Bo-102

POWER BLAST

Crest of Sincerity

EFFECT: Add 50 points to your Digimon Power. If you place this card on "Crest Tag" and you have Digivolved in this Duel, add an additional 50 points to your Digimon Power.

•Send this card Offline at end of Duel.

© Akiyoshi Hongo • Toei Animation   © 1999 BANDAI

☐ Crest of Sincerity

POWER OPTION Bo-103

POWER BLAST

Crest of Friendship

EFFECT: Add 50 points to your Digimon Power. If you place this card on "Crest Tag" and you win the Duel, add an additional 100 points to your score.

•Send this card Offline at end of Duel.

© Akiyoshi Hongo • Toei Animation   © 1999 BANDAI

☐ Crest of Friendship

POWER OPTION Bo-104

POWER BLAST

Black Gears

EFFECT: Add 100 points to your Digimon Power.

• Do not use this card with a Mega on Duel Zone.
• Send this card Offline at end of Duel.

© Akiyoshi Hongo • Toei Animation   © 1999 BANDAI

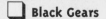

☐ Black Gears

POWER OPTION Bo-105

POWER BLAST

Flood

EFFECT: When confronting an opponent with Special Ability "Dig", add 50 points to your Digimon Power.

•Effect applies until voided by opponent or sent Offline by you.

© Akiyoshi Hongo • Toei Animation   © 1999 BANDAI

☐ Flood

POWER OPTION Bo-106

POWER BLAST

Meat

EFFECT: Add 20 points to your Digimon Power when your Digimon Group is Animal.

• Effect applies until voided by opponent or sent Offline by you.

© Akiyoshi Hongo • Toei Animation   © 1999 BANDAI

 Meat

POWER OPTION Bo-107

POWER BLAST

Waterproof

EFFECT: When your Digimon has Special Ability "Swim", add 100 points to your Digimon Power.

• Do not use this card with Rookie on Duel Zone.
• Send this card Offline at end of Duel.

© Akiyoshi Hongo • Toei Animation   © 1999 BANDAI

Waterproof

POWER OPTION Bo-108

POWER BLAST

Pluck

EFFECT: When confronting an opponent with Special Ability "Fly", score 200 points and continue Duel.

• Do not use this card with Rookie on Duel Zone.
• Send this card Offline at end of Duel.

© Akiyoshi Hongo • Toei Animation   © 1999 BANDAI

 Pluck